The Mind of the Artist

by Various

PREFACE

It is always interesting and profitable to get the views of workmen on their work, and on the principles which guide them in it; and in bringing together these sayings of artists Mrs. Binyon has done a very useful thing. A great number of opinions are presented, which, in their points of agreement and disagreement, bring before us in the most charming way the wide range of the artist's thought, and enable us to realise that the work of the great ones is not founded on vague caprice or so-called inspiration, but on sure intuitions which lead to definite knowledge; not merely the necessary knowledge of the craftsman, which many have possessed whose work has failed to hold the attention of the world, but also a knowledge of nature's laws.

"The Mind of the Artist" speaks for itself, and really requires no word of introduction. These opinions as a whole, seem to me to have a harmony and consistency, and to announce clearly that the directing impulse must be a desire for expression, that art is a language, and that the thing to be said is of more importance than the manner of saying it. This desire for expression is the driving-force of the artist; it informs, controls, and animates his method of working; it governs the hand and eye. That figures should give the impression of life and spontaneity, that the sun should shine, trees move in the wind, and nature be felt and represented as a living thing--this is the firm ground in art; and in those who have this feeling every effort will, consciously or unconsciously, lead towards its realisation. It should be the starting-point of the student. It does not absolve him from the need of taking the utmost pains, from making the most searching study of his model; rather it impels him, in the examination of whatever he feels called on to represent, to look for the vital and necessary things: and the artist will carry his work to the utmost degree of completion possible to him, in the desire to get at the heart of his theme.

"Truth to nature," like a wide mantle, shelters us all, and covers not only the outward aspect of things, but their inner meanings and the emotions felt through them, differently by each individual. And the inevitable differences of point of view, which one encounters in this book, are but small matters compared with the agreement one finds on essential things; I may instance particularly the stress laid on the observation of nature. Whether the artist chooses to depict the present, the past, or to express an abstract ideal, he must, if his work is to live, found it on his own experience of nature. But he must at every step also refer to the past. He must find the road that the great ones have made, remembering that the problems they solved were the same that he has before him, and that now, no less than in Duerer's time, "art is hidden in nature: it is for the artist to drag her forth."

GEORGE CLAUSEN.

NOTE

This little volume, it need hardly be said, does not aim at being complete, in the sense of representing all the artists who have written on art. It is hoped, however, that the sayings chosen will be found fairly representative of what painters and sculptors, typical of their race and time, have said about the various aspects of their work. In making the collection, I have had recourse less to famous comprehensive treatises and expositions of theory like those of Leonardo and of Reynolds, than to the more intimate avowals and working notes contained in letters and diaries, or recorded in memoirs. The selection of these has entailed considerable research; and in tracing what was often by no means easy to find, I wish to acknowledge the kind assistance, especially, of M. Raphael Petrucci, M. Louis Dimier, and Mr. Tancred Borenius. I have also to thank Lady Burne-Jones, Miss Birnie Philip, Mrs. Watts, Mrs. C. W. Furse, Mr. W. M. Rossetti, Mr. J. G. Millais, Mr. Samuel Calvert, and Mr. Sydney Cockerell, for permission to make quotations from Burne-Jones, Whistler, Watts, Furse, D. G. Rossetti, Madox Brown, Millais, Edward Calvert, and William Morris; also Sir Martin Conway, Sir Charles Holroyd, Mrs. Herringham, Mr. E. McCurdy, and Mr. Everard Meynell, for allowing me to use their translations from Duerer, Francisco d'Ollanda (conversations with Michael Angelo), Cennino Cennini, Leonardo, and Corot, respectively.

Thankful acknowledgment is also made to the authors of any other quotations whose names may inadvertently have been omitted.

Above all, I thank my husband for his advice and help.

C. M. B.

THE MIND OF THE ARTIST

I

An able painter by his power of penetration into the mysteries of his art is usually an able critic.

Alfred Stevens.[1]

[Footnote 1: The Belgian painter, not the English sculptor.]

II

Art, like love, excludes all competition, and absorbs the man.

Fuseli.

III

A good painter has two chief objects to paint, namely, man, and the intention of his soul. The first is easy, the second difficult, because he has to represent it through the attitudes and movements of the limbs. This should be learnt from the dumb, who do it better than any other sort of person.

Leonardo da Vinci.

IV

In my judgment that is the excellent and divine painting which is most like and best imitates any work of immortal God, whether a human figure, or a wild and strange animal, or a simple and easy fish, or a bird of the air, or any other creature. And this neither with gold nor silver nor with very fine tints, but drawn only with a pen or a pencil, or with a brush in black and white. To imitate perfectly each of these things in its species seems to me to be nothing else but to desire to imitate the work of immortal God. And yet that thing will be the most noble and perfect in the works of painting which in itself reproduced the thing which is most noble and of the greatest delicacy and knowledge.

Michael Angelo.

V

The art of painting is employed in the service of the Church, and by it the sufferings of Christ and many other profitable examples are set forth. It preserveth also the likeness of men after their death. By aid of delineations the measurements of the earth, the waters, and the stars are better to be understood; and many things likewise become known unto men by them. The attainment of true, artistic, and lovely execution in painting is hard to come unto; it needeth long time and a hand practised to almost perfect freedom. Whosoever, therefore, falleth short of this cannot attain a right understanding (in matters of painting) for it cometh alone by inspiration from above. The art of painting cannot be truly judged save by such as are themselves good painters; from others verily is it hidden even as a strange tongue. It were a noble occupation for ingenious youths without employment to exercise themselves in this art.

Duerer.

AIMS AND IDEALS

VI

Give thou to God no more than he asketh of thee; but to man also, that which is man's. In all that thou doest, work from thine own heart, simply; for his heart is as thine, when thine is wise and humble; and he shall have understanding of thee. One drop of rain is as another, and the sun's prism in all: and shalt not thou be as he, whose lives are the breath of One? Only by making thyself his equal can he learn to hold communion with thee, and at last own thee above him. Not till thou lean over the water shalt thou see thine image therein: stand erect, and it shall slope from thy feet and be lost. Know that there is but this means whereby thou mayst serve God with man.... Set thine hand and thy soul to serve man with God....

Chiaro, servant of God, take now thine Art unto thee, and paint me thus, as I am, to know me; weak, as I am, and in the weeds of this time; only with eyes which seek out labour, and with a faith, not learned, yet jealous of prayer. Do this; so shall thy soul stand before thee always, and perplex thee no more.

Rossetti.

VII

I know that this world is a world of imagination and vision. I see everything I paint in this world, but everybody does not see alike. To the eyes of a miser a guinea is far more beautiful than the sun, and a bag worn with the use of money has more beautiful proportions than a vine filled with grapes. The tree which moves some to tears of joy, is in the eyes of others only a green thing which stands in the way.... To the eye of the man of imagination, Nature is Imagination itself.

Blake.

VIII

Painting is nothing but the art of expressing the invisible by the visible.

Fromentin.

IX

The picture I speak of is a small one, and represents merely the figure of a woman, clad to the hands and feet with a green and grey raiment, chaste and early in its fashion, but exceedingly simple.

She is standing: her hands are held together lightly, and her eyes set earnestly open.

The face and hands in this picture, though wrought with great delicacy, have the appearance of being painted at once, in a single sitting: the drapery is unfinished. As soon as I saw the figure, it drew an awe upon me, like water in shadow. I shall not attempt to describe it more than I have already done, for the most absorbing wonder of it was its literality. You knew that figure, when painted, had been seen; yet it was not a thing to be seen of men.

Rossetti.

X

A great work of high art is a noble theme treated in a noble manner, awakening our best and most reverential feelings, touching our generosity, our tenderness, or disposing us generally to seriousness--a subject of human endurance, of human justice, of human aspiration and hope, depicted worthily by the special means art has in her power to use. In Michael Angelo and Raphael we have high art; in Titian we have high art; in Turner we have high art. The first appeals to our highest sensibilities by majesty of line, the second mainly by dignified serenity, the third by splendour especially, the Englishman by a combination of these qualities, but, lacking the directly human appeal to human sympathies, his work must be put on a lower level.

Watts.

XI

THE SIX CANONS OF ART

Rhythmic vitality, anatomical structure, conformity with nature, suitability of colouring, artistic composition, and finish.

Hsieh Ho (Chinese, sixth century A.D.).

XII

In painting, the most troublesome subject is man, then landscape, then dogs and horses, then buildings, which being fixed objects are easy to manage up to a certain point, but of which it is difficult to get finished pictures.

Ku K'ai-Chih (Chinese, fourth century A.D.).

XIII

First it is necessary to know what this sort of imitation is, and to define it.

Definition:

It is an imitation made with lines and with colours on some plane surface of everything that can be seen under the sun. Its object is to give delight.

Principles which may be learnt by all men of reason:

No visible object can be presented without light.

No visible object can be presented without a transparent medium.

No visible object can be presented without a boundary.

No visible object can be presented without colour.

No visible object can be presented without distance.

No visible object can be presented without an instrument.

What follows cannot be learnt, it is born with the painter.

Nicholas Poussin.

XIV

"In painting, and above all in portraiture," says Madame Cave in her charming essay, "it is soul which speaks to soul: and not knowledge which speaks to knowledge."

This observation, more profound perhaps than she herself was aware, is an arraignment of pedantry in execution. A hundred times I have said to myself, "Painting, speaking materially, is nothing but a bridge between the soul of the artist and that of the spectator."

Delacroix.

XV

The art of painting is perhaps the most indiscreet of all the arts. It is an unimpeachable witness to the moral state of the painter at the moment when he held the brush. The thing he willed to do he did: that which he only half-heartedly willed can be seen in his indecisions: that which he did not will at all is not to be found in his work, whatever he may say and whatever others may say. A distraction, a moment's forgetfulness, a glow of warmer feeling, a diminution of insight, relaxation of attention, a dulling of his love for what he is studying, the tediousness of painting and the passion for painting, all the shades of his nature, even to the lapses of his sensibility, all this is told by the painter's work as clearly as if he were telling it in our ears.

Fromentin.

XVI

The first merit of a picture is to feast the eyes. I don't mean that the intellectual element is not also necessary; it is as with fine poetry ... all the intellect in the world won't prevent it from being bad if it grates harshly on the ear. We talk of having an ear; so it is not every eye which is fitted to enjoy the subtleties of painting. Many people have a false eye or an indolent eye; they can see objects literally, but the exquisite is beyond them.

Delacroix.

XVII

I would like my work to appeal to the eye and mind as music appeals to the ear and heart. I have something that I want to say which may be useful to and touch mankind, and to say it as well as I can in form and colour is my endeavour; more than that I cannot do.

Watts.

XVIII

Give me leave to say, that to paint a very beautiful Woman, I ought to have before me those that are the most so; with this Condition, that your Lordship might assist me in choosing out the greatest Beauty. But as I am under a double Want, both of good Judgment and fine Women, I am forced to go by a certain Idea which I form in my own Mind. Whether this hath any Excellence of Art in it, I cannot determine; but 'tis what I labour at.

Raphael.

XIX

I mean by a picture a beautiful romantic dream of something that never was, never will be--in a light better than any light that ever shone--in a land no one can define or remember, only desire--and the forms divinely beautiful--and then I wake up with the waking of Brynhild.

Burne-Jones.

XX

I love everything for what it is.

Courbet.

XXI

I look for my tones; it is quite simple.

Courbet.

XXII

Many people imagine that art is capable of an indefinite progress toward perfection. This is a mistake. There is a limit where it must stop. And for this reason: the conditions which govern the imitation of nature are fixed. The object is to produce a picture, that is to say, a plane surface either with or without a border, and on this surface the representation of something produced by the sole means of different colouring substances. Since it is obliged to remain thus circumscribed, it is easy to foresee the limit of perfectibility. When the picture has succeeded in satisfying our minds in all the conditions imposed on its production, it will cease to interest. Such is the fate of everything which has attained its end: we grow indifferent and abandon it.

In the conditions governing the production of the picture, every means has been explored. The most difficult problem was that of complete relief, depth of perspective carried to the point of perfect illusion. The stereoscope has solved the problem. It only remains now to combine this perfection with the other kinds of perfection already found. Let no man imagine that art, bound by these conditions of the plane surface, can ever free itself from the circle which limits it. It is easy to foresee that its last word will soon have been said.

Wiertz.

XXIII

In his admirable book on Shakespeare, Victor Hugo has shown that there is no progress in the arts. Nature, their model, is unchangeable; and the arts cannot transcend her limits. They attain completeness of expression in the work of a master, on whom other masters are formed. Then comes development, and then a lapse, an interval. By-and-by, art is born anew under the stimulus of a man who catches from Light a new convention.

Bracquemond.

XXIV

The painter ... does not set his palette with the real hues of the rainbow. When he pictures to us the character of a hero, or paints some scene of nature, he does not present us with a living man in the character of the hero (for this is the business of dramatic art); nor does he make up his landscape of real rocks, or trees, or water, but with fictitious resemblances of these. Yet in these figments he is as truly bound by the laws of the appearance of those realities, of which they are the copy (and very much to the same extent), as the musician is by the natural laws and properties of sound.

In short, the whole object of physical science, or, in other words, the whole of sensible nature, is included in the domain of imitative art, either as the subjects, the objects, or the materials of imitation: every fine art, therefore, has certain physical sciences collateral to it, on the abstractions of which it builds, more or less, according to its nature and purpose. But the drift of the art itself is something totally distinct from that of the physical science to which it is related; and it is not more absurd to say that physiology or anatomy constitute the science of poetry or dramatic art than that acoustics and harmonics are the science of music; optics, of painting; mechanics, or other branches of physical science, that of architecture.

Dyce.

XXV

After all I have seen of Art, with nothing am I more impressed than with the necessity, in all great work, for suppressing the workman and all the mean dexterity of practice. The result itself, in quiet dignity, is the only worthy attainment. Wood-engraving, of all things most ready for dexterity, reads us a good lesson.

Edward Calvert.

XXVI

Shall Painting be confined to the sordid drudgery of facsimile representations of merely mortal and perishing substances, and not be as poetry and music are, elevated into its own proper sphere of invention and visionary conception? No, it shall not be so! Painting, as well as poetry and music, exists and exults in immortal thoughts.

Blake.

XXVII

If any man has any poetry in him, he should paint, for it has all been said and written, and they have scarcely begun to paint it.

William Morris.

XXVIII

Long live conscience and simplicity! there lies the only way to the true and the sublime.

Corot.

XXIX

All the young men of this school of Ingres have something of the pedant about them; they seem to think that merely to be enrolled among the party of serious painters is a merit in itself. Serious painting is their party cry. I told Demay that a crowd of people of talent had done nothing worth speaking of because of all these factious dogmas that they get enslaved to, or that the prejudice of the moment imposes on them. So, for example, with this famous cry of Beauty, which is, according to the world's opinion, the goal of the arts: if it is the one and only goal, what becomes of men who, like Rubens, Rembrandt, and northern natures in general, prefer other qualities? Demand of Puget purity, beauty in fact, and it is good-bye to his verve. Speaking generally, men of the North are less attracted to beauty; the Italian prefers decoration; this applies to music too.

Delacroix.

XXX

At the present time the task is easier. It is a question of allowing to everything its own interest, of putting man back in his place, and, if need be, of doing without him. The moment has come to think less, to aim less high, to look more closely, to observe better, to paint as well but differently. This is the painting of the crowd, of the townsman, the workman, the parvenu, the man in the street; done wholly for him, done from him. It is a question of becoming humble before humble things, small before small things, subtle before subtle things; of gathering them all together without omission and without disdain, of entering familiarly into their intimacy, affectionately into their way of being; it is a matter of sympathy, attentive curiosity, patience. Henceforth, genius will consist in having no prejudice, in not being conscious of one's knowledge, in allowing oneself to be taken by surprise by one's model, in asking only from him how he shall be represented. As for beautifying--never! ennobling--never! correcting--never! These are lies and useless trouble. Is there not in every artist worthy of the name a something which sees to this naturally and without effort?

Fromentin.

XXXI

I send you also some etchings and a "Woman drinking Absinthe," drawn this winter from life in Paris. It is a girl called Marie Joliet, who used every evening to come drunk to the Bal Bullier, and who had a look in her eyes of death galvanised into life. I made her sit to me and tried to render what I saw. This is my principle in the task I have set before me. I am determined to make no book illustration but it shall be a means of contributing towards an effect of life and nothing more. A patch of colour and it is sufficient; we must leave these childish thoughts behind us. Life! we must try to render life, and it is hard enough.

Felicien Rops.

XXXII

So this damned Realism made an instinctive appeal to my painter's vanity, and deriding all traditions, cried aloud with the confidence of ignorance, "Back to Nature!" Nature! ah, my friend, what mischief that cry has done me. Where was there an apostle apter to receive this doctrine, so convenient for me as it was--beautiful Nature, and all that humbug? It is nothing but that. Well, the world was watching; and it saw "The Piano," the "White Girl," the Thames subjects, the marines ... canvases produced by a fellow who was puffed up with the conceit of being able to prove to his comrades his magnificent gifts, qualities which only needed a rigorous training to make their possessor to-day a master, instead of a dissipated student. Ah, why was I not a pupil of Ingres? I don't say that out of enthusiasm for his pictures; I have only a moderate liking for them. Several of his canvases, which we have looked at together, seem to me of a very questionable style, not at all Greek, as people want to call it, but French, and viciously French. I feel that we must go far beyond this, that there are far more beautiful things to be done. Yet, I repeat, why was I not his pupil? What a master he would have been for us! How salutary would have been his guidance!

Whistler.

XXXIII

It has been said, "Who will deliver us from the Greeks and Romans?" Soon we shall be saying, "Who will deliver us from realism?" Nothing is so tiring as a constant close imitation of life. One comes back inevitably to imaginative work. Homer's fictions will always be preferred to historical truth, Rubens' fabulous magnificence to all the frippery copied exactly from the lay figure.

The painter who is a machine will pass away, the painter who is a mind will remain; the spirit for ever triumphs over matter.

Wiertz.

XXXIV

A little book by the Russian soldier and artist Verestchagin is interesting to the student. As a realist, he condemns all art founded on the principles of picture-makers, and depends only on exact imitation, and the conditions of accident. In our seeking after truth, and endeavour never to be unreal or affected, it must not be forgotten that this endeavour after truth is to be made with materials altogether unreal and different from the object to be imitated. Nothing in a picture is real; indeed, the painter's art is the most unreal thing in the whole range of our efforts. Though art must be founded on nature, art and nature are distinctly different things; in a certain class of subjects probability may, indeed must, be violated, provided the violation is not disagreeable.

Everything in a work of art must accord. Though gloom and desolation would deepen the effects of a distressing incident in real life, such accompaniments are not necessary to make us feel a thrill of horror or awaken the keenest sympathy. The most awful circumstances may take place under the purest sky, and amid the most lovely surroundings. The human sensibilities will be too much affected by the human sympathies to heed the external conditions; but to awaken in a picture similar impressions, certain artificial aids must be used; the general aspect must be troubled or sad.

Watts.

XXXV

The remarks made on my "Man with the Hoe" seem always very strange to me, and I am obliged to you for repeating them to me, for once more it sets me marvelling at the ideas they impute to me. In what club have my critics ever encountered me? A Socialist, they cry! Well, really, I might answer the charge as the commissary from Auvergne did when he wrote home: "They have been saying that I am a Saint-Simonian: it's not true; I don't know what a

Saint-Simonian is."

Can't they then simply admit such ideas as may occur to the mind in looking at a man doomed to gain his living by the sweat of his brow? There are some who tell me that I deny the charm of the country. I find in the country much more than charm; I find infinite splendour; I look on everything as they do on the little powers of which Christ said, "I say unto you, that Solomon in all his glory was not arrayed like one of these." I see and note the aureole on the dandelion, and the sun which, far away, beyond the stretching country, spends his glory on the clouds. I see just as much in the flat plain; in the horses steaming as they toil; and then in a stony place I see a man quite exhausted, whose gasps have been audible since morning, who tries to draw himself up for a moment to take breath. The drama is surrounded by splendours. This is no invention of mine; and it is long since that expression "the cry of the earth" was discovered. My critics are men of learning and taste, I imagine; but I cannot put myself into their skins, and since I have never in my life seen anything but the fields, I try to tell, as best I can, what I have seen and experienced as I worked.

Millet.

XXXVI

One of the hardest things in the world is to determine how much realism is allowable in any particular picture. It is of so many different kinds too. For instance, I want a shield or a crown or a pair of wings or what not, to look real. Well, I make what I want, or a model of it, and then make studies from that. So that what eventually gets on to the canvas is a reflection of a reflection of something purely imaginary. The three Magi never had crowns like that, supposing them to have had crowns at all, but the effect is realistic because the crown from which the studies were made is real--and so on.

Burne-Jones.

XXXVII

Do you understand now that all my intelligence rejects is in immediate relation to all my heart aspires to, and that the spectacle of human blunders and human vileness is an equally powerful motive for action in the exercise of art with springs of tranquil contemplation that I have felt within me since I was a child?

We have come far, I hope, from the shadowy foliage crowning the humble roof of the primitive human dwelling, far from the warbling of the birds that brood among the branches; far from all these tender things. We left them, notwithstanding, the other day; and even if we had stayed, do you think we should have continued to enjoy them?

Believe me, everything comes from the universal; we must embrace to give life.

Whatever interest one may get from material offered by a period, religion, manners, history, &c., in representing a particular type, it will avail nothing without an understanding of the universal agency of atmosphere, that modelling of infinity; it shall come to pass that a stone fence, about which the air seems to move and breathe, shall be, in a museum, a grander conception than any ambitious work which lacks this universal element and expresses only something personal. All the personal and particular majesty of a portrait of Louis XIV. by Lebrun or by Rigaud shall be as nothing beside the simplicity of a tuft of grass shining clear in a gleam of sunlight.

Rousseau.

XXXVIII

Of all the things that is likely to give us back popular art in England, the cleaning of England is the first and the most necessary. Those who are to make beautiful things must live in a beautiful place.

William Morris.

XXXIX

On the whole, one must suppose that beauty is a marketable quality, and that the better the work is all round, both as a work of art and in its technique, the more likely it is to find favour with the public.

William Morris.

ART AND SOCIETY

XL

With the language of beauty in full resonance around him, art was not difficult to the painter and sculptor of old as it is with us. No anatomical study will do for the modern artist what habitual acquaintance with the human form did for Pheidias. No Venetian painted a horse with the truth and certainty of Horace Vernet, who knew the animal by heart, rode him, groomed him, and had him constantly in his studio. Every artist must paint what he sees, rather every artist must paint what is around him, can produce no great work unless he impress the character of his age upon his production, not necessarily taking his subjects from it (better if he can), but taking the impress of its life. The great art of Pheidias did not deal with the history of his time, but compressed into its form the qualities of the most intellectual period the world has seen; nor were any materials to be invented or borrowed, he had them all at hand, expressing himself in a natural language derived from familiarity with natural objects. Beauty is the language of art, and with this at command thoughts as they arise take visible form perhaps almost without effort, or (certain technical difficulties overcome) with little more than is required in writing--this not absolving the artist or the poet from earnest thought and severe study. In many respects the present age is far more advanced than preceding times, incomparably more full of knowledge;

but the language of great art is dead, for general, noble beauty, pervades life no more. The artist is obliged to return to extinct forms of speech if he would speak as the great ones have spoken. Nothing beautiful is seen around him, excepting always sky and trees and sea; these, as he is mainly a dweller in cities, he cannot live enough with. But it is, perhaps, in the real estimation in which art is held that we shall find the reason for failure. If the world cared for her language, art could not help speaking, the utterance being, perhaps, simply beautiful. But even in these days when we have ceased to prize this, if it were demanded that art should take its place beside the great intellectual outflow of the time, the response would hardly be doubtful.

Watts.

XLI

You refer to the use and purpose of the liberal arts; not a city in Europe, at present, is fulfilling them. And if any one in Melbourne were now to produce, even on a small scale, a picture fulfilling the conditions of liberal art, then Melbourne might take the lead of civilised cities. But it is not the ambition of leading, nor the restlessness of a competitive spirit that may accomplish this.

A good poem, whether painted or written, whether large or small, should represent beautiful life. Are you able to name any one who has conceived this beauty of the life of men? I will not complicate the requirements of painted poesy by speaking of the music of colour with which it should be clothed; black and white were enough. The very attempt to express the confession of love were fulfilment sufficient.

Edward Calvert.

XLII

So art has become foolishly confounded with education, that all should be equally qualified. Whereas, while polish, refinement, culture, and breeding are in no way arguments for artistic result, it is also no reproach to the most finished scholar or greatest gentleman in the land that he be absolutely without eye for painting or ear for music--that in his heart he prefer the popular print to the scratch of Rembrandt's needle, or the songs of the hall to Beethoven's "C Minor Symphony."

Let him have but the wit to say so, and not let him feel the admission a proof of inferiority.

Art happens--no hovel is safe from it, no prince may depend on it, the vastest intelligence cannot bring it about, and puny efforts to make it universal end in quaint comedy and coarse farce.

This is as it should be; and all attempts to make it otherwise are due to the eloquence of the ignorant, the zeal of the conceited.

Whistler.

XLIII

Art will not grow and flourish, nay it will not long exist, unless it be shared by all people; and for my part I don't wish that it should.

William Morris.

XLIV

No, art is not an element of corruption. The man who drinks from a wooden bowl is nearer to the brute that drinks from a stone trough than he who quenches his thirst from a crystal cup; and the artist who gave the glass its shape, impressed as in a mould of bronze by the simple means of a second's breath and yet more cheaply than the fashioning of the wooden bowl, has done more to ennoble and improve his neighbour than any inventor of a system: in his work he gives him the use and the enjoyment of things for which orators can only create a craving.

Jules Klagmann.

XLV

The improviser never makes fine poetry.

Titian.

XLVI

Agatharcus said to Zeuxis--For my part I soon despatch my Pictures. You are a happy Man, replies Zeuxis; I do mine with Time and application, because I would have them good, and I am satisfyed, that what is soon done, will soon be forgotten.

XLVII

Art is not a pleasure trip. It is a battle, a mill that grinds.

Millet.

STUDY AND TRAINING

XLVIII

Raphael and Michael Angelo owe that immortal fame of theirs, which has gone out into the ends of the earth, to the passion of curiosity and delight with which this noble subject inspired them.

No man who has not studied the sciences can make a work that shall bring him great praise, save from ignorant and easily satisfied persons.

Jean Goujon.

XLIX

He that would be a painter must have a natural turn thereto.

Love and delight therein are better teachers of the Art of Painting than compulsion is.

If a man is to become a really good painter he must be educated thereto from his very earliest years. He must copy much of the work of good artists until he attain a free hand.

To paint is to be able to portray upon a flat surface any visible thing whatsoever that may be chosen.

It is well for any one first to learn how to divide and reduce to measure the human figure, before learning anything else.

Duerer.

L

The painter requires such knowledge of mathematics as belongs to painting, and severance from companions who are not in sympathy with his studies, and his brain should have the power of adapting itself to the tenor of the objects which present themselves before it, and he should be freed from all other cares. And if, while considering and examining one subject, a second should intervene, as happens when an object occupies the mind, he ought to decide which of these subjects presents greater difficulties in investigation, and follow that until it becomes entirely clear, and afterwards pursue the investigation of the other. And above all he should keep his mind as clear as the surface of a mirror, which becomes changed to as many different colours as are those of the objects within it, and his companions should resemble him in a taste for these studies; and if he fail to find any such, he should accustom himself to be alone in his investigations, for in the end he will find no more profitable companionship.

Leonardo.

LI

If you are fond of copying other Men's Work, as being Originals more constant to be seen and imitated than any living Object, I should rather advise to copy anything moderately carved than excellently painted: For by imitating a Picture, we only habituate our Hand to take a mere Resemblance; whereas by drawing from a carved Original, we learn not only to take this Resemblance, but also the true Lights.

Leon Battista Alberti.

LII

There are a thousand proofs that the old masters and all good painters from Raphael onwards executed their frescoes from cartoons and their little easel pictures from more or less finished drawings.... Your model gives you exactly what you want to paint neither in character of drawing nor in colour, but at the same time you cannot do without him.

To paint Achilles the most goodly of men, though you had for your model the most abject you must depend on him, and can depend on him for the structure of the human body, for its movement and poise. The proof of this is that Raphael used his pupils in his studies for the movements of the figures in his divine pictures.

Whatever your talents may be, if you paint not from your studies after nature, but directly from the model, you will always be a slave and your pictures will show it. Raphael, on the contrary, had so completely mastered nature and had his mind so full of her, that instead of being ruled by her, one might say that she obeyed him and came at his command to place herself in his pictures.

Ingres.

LIII

No one can ever design till he has learned the language of Art by making many finished copies both of Nature, Art, and of whatever comes in his way, from earliest childhood. The difference between a bad artist and a good is, that the bad artist seems to copy a great deal, the good one does copy a great deal.

Blake.

LIV

If you deprive an artist of all he has borrowed from the experience of others the originality left will be but a twentieth part of him.

Originality by itself cannot constitute a remarkable talent.

Wiertz.

LV

I am convinced that to reach the highest degree of perfection as a painter, it is necessary, not only to be acquainted with the ancient statues, but we must be inwardly imbued with a thorough comprehension of them.

Rubens.

LVI

First of all copy drawings by a good master made by his art from nature and not as exercises; then from a relief, keeping by you a drawing done from the same relief; then from a good model, and of this you ought to make a practice.

Leonardo.

LVII

I wish to do something purely Greek; I feed my eyes on the antique statues, I mean even to imitate some of them. The Greeks never scrupled to reproduce a composition, a movement, a type already received and used. They put all their care, all their art, into perfecting an idea which had been used by others before them. They thought, and thought rightly, that in the arts the manner of rendering and expressing an idea matters more than the idea itself.

To give a clothing, a perfect form to one's thought is to be an artist ... it is the only way.

Well, I have done my best and I hope to attain my object.

L. David.

LVIII

Who amongst us, if he were to attempt in reality to represent a celebrated work of Apelles or Timanthus, such as Pliny describes them, but would produce something absurd, or perfectly foreign to the exalted greatness of the ancients? Each one, relying on his own powers, would produce some wretched, crude, unfermented stuff, instead of an exquisite old wine, uniting strength and mellowness, outraging those great spirits whom I endeavour reverently to follow, satisfied, however, to honour the marks of their footsteps, instead of supposing--I acknowledge it candidly--that I can ever attain to their eminence even in mere conception.

Rubens.

LIX

[You have stated that you thought these Marbles had great truth and imitation of nature; do you consider that that adds to their value?]

It considerably adds to it, because I consider them as united with grand form. There is in them that variety that is produced in the human form, by the alternate action and repose of the muscles, that strike one particularly. I have myself a very good collection of the best casts from the antique statues, and was struck with that difference in them, in returning from the Elgin Marbles to my own house.

Lawrence.

LX

It is absolutely necessary that at some moment or other in one's career one should reach the point, not of despising all that is outside oneself, but of abandoning for ever that almost blind fanaticism which impels us all to imitate the great masters, and to swear only by their works. It is necessary to say to oneself, That is good for Rubens, this for Raphael, Titian, or Michael Angelo. What they have done is their own business; I am not bound to this master or to that. It is necessary to learn to make what one has found one's own: a pinch of personal inspiration is worth everything else.

Delacroix.

LXI

From Phidias to Clodion, from Correggio to Fragonard, from the greatest to the least of those who have deserved the name of master, Art has been pursuing the Chimaera, attempting to reconcile two opposites--the most slavish fidelity to nature and the most absolute independence of her, an independence so absolute that the work of art may claim to be a creation. This is the persistent problem offered by the unstable character of the point of view at which it is approached; the whole mystery of art. The subject, as presented in nature, cannot keep the place which art with its transforming instinct would assign it; and therefore a single formula can never be adequate to the totality of nature's manifestations; the draughtsman will talk of its form, a colourist of its effect.

Considered in this light, nature is nothing more than one of the instruments of the arts, in the same category with their principles, elements, formulas, conventions, tools.

Bracquemond.

LXII

One must copy nature always, and learn how to see her rightly. It is for this that one should study the antique and the great masters, not in order to imitate them, but, I repeat, to learn to see.

Do you think I send you to the Louvre to find there what people call "le beau ideal," something which is outside nature?

It was stupidity like this which in bad periods led to the decadence of art. I send you there to learn from the antique how to see nature, because they themselves are nature: therefore one must live among them, and absorb them.

It is the same in the painting of the great ages. Do you think, when I tell you to copy, that I want to make copyists of you? No, I want you to take the sap from the plant.

Ingres.

LXIII

The strict copying of nature is not art; it is only a means to an end, an element in the whole. Art, while presenting nature, must manifest itself in its own essence. It is not a mirror, uncritically reflecting every image; it is the artist who must mould the image to his will; else his work is not performed.

Bracquemond.

LXIV

Nature contains the elements, in colour and form, of all pictures, as the keyboard contains the notes of all music. But the artist is born to pick, and choose, and group with science, these elements, that the result may be beautiful; as the musician gathers his notes, and forms his chords, until he bring forth from chaos glorious harmony.

To say to the painter that Nature is to be taken as she is, is to say to the player that he may sit on the piano.

Whistler.

LXV

When you have thoroughly learnt perspective, and have fixed in your memory all the various parts and forms of things, you should often amuse yourself when you take a walk for recreation, in watching and taking note of the attitudes and actions of men as they talk and dispute, or laugh or come to blows one with another, both their actions and those of the bystanders who either intervene or stand looking on at these things; noting these down with rapid strokes in this way, in a little pocket-book, which you ought always to carry with you. And let this be of tinted paper, so that it may not be rubbed out; but you should change the old for a new one, for these are not things to be rubbed out but preserved with the utmost diligence; for there is such an infinite number of forms and actions of things that the memory is incapable of preserving them, and therefore you should keep those (sketches) as your patterns and teachers.

Leonardo.

LXVI

Two men stop to talk together: I pencil them in detail, beginning at the head, for example; they separate and I have nothing but a fragment on my paper. Some children are sitting on the steps of a church; I begin, their mother calls them; my sketch-book becomes filled with tips of noses and locks of hair. I make a resolution not to go home without a whole figure, and I try for the first time to draw in mass, to draw rapidly, which is the only possible way of drawing, and which is to-day one of the chief faculties of our moderns. I put myself to draw in the winking of an eye the first group that presents itself; if it moves on I have at least put down the general character; if it stops, I can go on to the details. I do many such exercises, and have even gone so far as to cover the lining of my hat with lightning sketches of opera-ballets and opera scenery.

Corot.

LXVII

There is my model (the artist pointed to the crowd which thronged a market-place); art lives by studying nature, not by imitating any artist.

Eupompus.

LXVIII

When you have clearly and distinctly learned in what good colouring consists, you cannot do better than have recourse to nature herself, who is always at hand, and in comparison of whose true splendour the best coloured pictures are but faint and feeble.

However, as the practice of copying is not entirely to be excluded, since the mechanical practice of painting is learned in some measure by it, let those choice parts only be selected which have recommended the work to notice. If its excellence consists in its general effect, it would be proper to make slight sketches of the machinery and general management of the picture. Those sketches should be kept always by you for the regulation of your style. Instead of copying the touches of those great masters, copy only their conceptions. Instead of treading in their footsteps, endeavour only to keep the same road. Labour to invent on their general principles and way of thinking. Possess yourself with their spirit. Consider with yourself how a Michael Angelo or a Raffaelle would have treated this subject; and work yourself into a belief that your picture is to be seen and criticised by them when completed. Even an attempt of this kind will rouse your powers.

Reynolds.

LXIX

What do you mean--that you have been working, but without success? Do you mean that you cannot get the price you ask? then sell it for less, till, by practice, you shall improve, and command a better price. Or do you only mean that you are not satisfied with your work? nobody ever was that I know, except J---- W----. Peg away! While you're at work you must be improving. Do something from Nature indoors when you cannot get out, to keep your hand and eye in practice. Don't get into the way of working too much at your drawings away from Nature.

Charles Keene.

LXX

The purpose of art is no other than to delineate the form and express the spirit of an object, animate or inanimate, as the case may be. The use of art is to produce copies of things; and if an artist has a thorough knowledge of the properties of the thing he paints he can assuredly make a name. Just as a writer of profound erudition and good memory has ever at his command an inexhaustible supply of words and phrases which he freely makes use of in writing, so can a painter, who has accumulated experience by drawing from nature, paint any object without a conscious effort. The artist who confines himself to copying from models painted by his master, fares no better than a literatus who cannot rise above transcribing others' compositions. An ancient critic says that writing ends in describing a thing or narrating an event, but painting can represent the actual forms of things. Without the true depiction of objects, there can be no pictorial art. Nobility of sentiment and such-like only come after a successful delineation of the external form of an object. The beginner in art should direct his efforts more to the latter than to the former. He should learn to paint according to his own ideas, not to slavishly copy the models of old artists. Plagiarism is a crime to be avoided not only by men of letters but also by painters.

Okio (Japanese, eighteenth century).

LXXI

I remember Duerer the painter, who used to say that, as a young man, he loved extraordinary and unusual designs in painting, but that in his old age he took to examining Nature, and strove to imitate her as closely as he possibly could; but he found by experience how hard it is not to deviate from her.

Duerer (quoted by Melancthon).

LXXII

I have heard painters acknowledge, though in that acknowledgment no degradation of themselves was intended, that they could do better without Nature than with her; or, as they expressed it themselves, that it only put them out. A painter with such ideas and such habits, is indeed in a most hopeless state. The art of seeing Nature, or, in other words, the art of using models, is in reality the great object, the point to which all our studies are directed. As for the power of being able to do tolerably well, from practice alone, let it be valued according to its worth. But I do not see in what manner it can be sufficient for the production of correct, excellent, and finished pictures. Works deserving this character never were produced, nor ever will arise, from memory alone; and I will venture to say, that an artist who brings to his work a mind tolerably furnished with the general principles of art, and a taste formed upon the works of good artists, in short, who knows in what excellence consists, will, with the assistance of models, which we will likewise suppose he has learnt the art of using, be an over-match for the greatest painter that ever lived who should be debarred such advantages.

Reynolds.

LXXIII

Do not imitate; do not follow others--you will always be behind them.

Corot.

LXXIV

Never paint a subject unless it calls insistently and distinctly upon your eye and heart.

Corot.

LXXV

I should never paint anything that was not the result of an impression received from the aspect of nature, whether in landscape or figures.

Millet.

LXXVI

You must interpret nature with entire simplicity and according to your personal sentiment, altogether detaching yourself from what you know of the old masters or of contemporaries. Only in this way will you do work of real feeling. I know gifted people who will not avail themselves of their power. Such people seem to me like a billiard-player whose adversary is constantly giving him good openings, but who makes no use of them. I think that if I were playing with that man, I would say, "Very well, then, I will give you no more." If I were to sit in judgment, I would punish the miserable creatures who squander their natural gifts, and I would turn their hearts to work.

Corot.

LXXVII

Sensation is rude and false unless informed by intellection; and, however delicate be the touch in obedience to remote gradation, yet knowledge of the genus necessarily invests the representation with perspicuous and truthful relations that ignorance could not possibly have observed. Hence--Paint what you see; but know what you see.

Only paint what you love in what you see, and discipline yourself to separate this essence from its dumb accompaniments, so that the accents fall upon the points of passion. Let that which must be expressed of the rest be merged, syncopated in the largeness of the modulation.

Boldly dare to omit the impertinent or irrelevant, and let the features of the passion be modulated in fewness.

Not a touch without its meaning or its significance throughout the courses. There is no disgrace, but on the contrary, honour, be the touches never so few, if studied. By determined refusal to touch vaguely, and with persistence in the slowness of thoughtful work, a noble style may be at length obtained: swift as sublime.

Edward Calvert.

LXXVIII

I started on Monday, 25th August, for Honfleur, where I stayed till 5th September in the most blessed condition of spirit.

There I worked with my head, with my eyes, harvesting effects in the mind; then, going over everything again, I called up within myself the figures desired for the completion of the composition. Once I had evoked all this world from nothingness, and envisaged it, and had found where each thing was to be, I had to return to Paris to ask for nature's authorisation and make sure of my advance. Nature justified me, and, as she is kind to those who approach her reverentially, gave me of her grace without stint.

Puvis de Chavannes.

LXXIX

I wish to tell you, Francisco d'Ollanda, of an exceedingly great beauty in this science of ours, of which perhaps you are aware, and which, I think, you consider the highest, namely, that what one has most to work and struggle for in painting, is to do the work with a great amount of labour and study in such a way that it may afterwards appear, however much it was laboured, to have been done almost quickly and almost without any labour, and very easily, although it was not. And this is a very excellent beauty. At times some things are done with little work in the way I have said, but very seldom; most are done by dint of hard work and appear to have been done very quickly.

Michael Angelo.

METHODS OF WORK

LXXX

Every successful work is rapidly performed; quickness is only execrable when it is empty--small. No one condemns the swiftness of an eagle.

To him who knows not the burden of process--the attributes that are to claim attention with every epocha of the performance--all attempt at swiftness will be mere pretence.

Edward Calvert.

LXXXI

I am planning a large picture, and I regard all you say, but I do not enter into that notion of varying one's plans to keep the public in good humour. Change of weather and effect will always afford variety. What if Van der Velde had quitted his sea-pieces, or Ruysdael his waterfalls, or Hobbema his native woods? The world would have lost so many features in art. I know that you wish for no material alteration, but I have to combat from high quarters-- even from Lawrence--the plausible argument that subject makes the picture. Perhaps you think an evening effect might do; perhaps it might start me some new admirers, but I should lose many old ones. I imagine myself driving a nail; I have driven it some way, and by persevering I may drive it home; by quitting it to attack others, though I may amuse myself, I do not advance beyond the first, while that particular nail stands still. No man who can do any one thing well will be able to do any other different thing equally well; and this is true of Shakespeare, the greatest master of variety.

Constable.

LXXXII

To work on the Ladye. Found part of the drapery bad, rubbed it out, heightened the seat she sits on, mended the heads again; did a great deal, but not finished yet. Any one might be surprised to read how I work whole days on an old drawing done many years since, and which I have twice worked over since it was rejected from the Royal Academy in '47, and now under promise of sale to White for L20. But I cannot help it. When I see a work going out of my hands, it is but natural, if I see some little defect, that I should try to mend it, and what follows is out of my power to direct: if I give one touch to a head, I give myself three days' work, and spoil it half-a-dozen times over.

Ford Madox Brown.

LXXXIII

In literature as in art the rough sketches of the masters are made for connoisseurs, not for the vulgar crowd.

A. Preault.

LXXXIV

It is true sketches, or such drawings as painters generally make for their works, give this pleasure of imagination to a high degree. From a slight, undetermined drawing, where the ideas of the composition and character are, as I may say, only just touched upon, the imagination supplies more than the painter himself, probably, could produce; and we accordingly often find that the finished work disappoints the expectation that was raised from the sketch; and this power of the imagination is one of the causes of the great pleasure we have in viewing a collection of drawings by great painters.

Reynolds.

LXXXV

I have just been examining all the sketches I have used in making this work. How many there are which fully satisfied me at the beginning, and which seem feeble, inadequate, or ill-composed, now that the paintings are advanced. I cannot tell myself often enough that it means an immense deal of labour to bring a work to the highest pitch of impressiveness of which it is capable. The oftener I revise it, the more it will gain in expressiveness.... Though the touch disappear, though the fire of execution be no longer the chief merit of the painting, there is no doubt about this; and again how often does it happen that after this intense labour, which has turned one's thought back on itself in every direction, the hand obeys more swiftly and surely in giving the desired lightness to the last touches.

Delacroix.

LXXXVI

Let us agree as to the meaning of the word "finished." What finishes a picture is not the quantity of detail in it, but the rightness of the general effect. A picture is not limited only by its frame. Whatever be the subject, there must be a principal object on which your eyes rest continually: the other objects are only the complement of this, they are less interesting to you; and after that there is nothing more for your eye.

There is the real limit of your picture. This principal object must seem so to the spectator of your work. Therefore, one must always return to this, and state its colour with more and more decision.

Rousseau.

LXXXVII

ON PROTOGENES

He was a great Master, but he often spoil'd his Pieces by endeavouring to make them Perfect; he did not know when he had done well; a Man may do too much as well as too little; and he is truly skilful, who knew what was sufficient.

Apelles.

FINISH

LXXXVIII

A picture must always be a little spoilt in the finishing of it. The last touches, which are intended to draw the picture together, take off from its freshness. To appear before the public one must cut out all those happy accidents which are the joy of the artist. I compare these murderous retouchings to those banal flourishes with which all airs of music end, and to those insignificant spaces which the musician is forced to put between the interesting parts of his work in order to lead on from one motive to another or to give them their proper value.

Re-touching, however, is not so fatal to a picture as one might think, when the picture has been well thought out and worked at with deep feeling. Time, in effacing the touches, old as well as new, gives back to the work its complete effect.

Delacroix.

LXXXIX

A picture, the effect of which is true, is finished.

Goya.

XC

You please me much, by saying that no other fault is found in your picture than the roughness of the surface; for that part being of use in giving force to the effect at a proper distance, and what a judge of painting knows an original from a copy by--in short, being the touch of the pencil which is harder to preserve than smoothness, I am much better pleased that they should spy out things of that kind, than to see an eye half an inch out of its place, or a nose out of drawing when viewed at a proper distance. I don't think it would be more ridiculous for a person to put his nose close to the canvas and say the colours smelt offensive, than to say how rough the paint lies; for one is just as material as the other with regard to hurting the effect and drawing of a picture.

Gainsborough.

XCI

The picture[2] will be seen to the greatest advantage if it is hung in a strong light, and in such a manner that the spectator can stand at some distance from it.

Rembrandt.

[Footnote 2: Probably the "Blinding of Samson."]

XCII

Don't look at a picture close, it smells bad.

Rembrandt.

XCIII

Try to be frank in drawing and in colour; give things their full relief; make a painting which can be seen at a distance; this is indispensable.

Chasseriau.

XCIV

If I might point out to you another defect, very prevalent of late, in our pictures, and one of the same contracted character with those you so happily illustrate, it would be that of the want of breadth, and in others a perpetual division and subdivision of parts, to give what their perpetrators call space; add to this a constant disturbing and torturing of everything whether in light or in shadow, by a niggling touch, to produce fulness of subject. This is the very reverse of what we see in Cuyp or Wilson, and even, with all his high finishing, in Claude. I have been warning our friend Collins against this, and was also urging young Landseer to beware of it; and in what I have been doing lately myself have been studying much from Rembrandt and from Cuyp, so as to acquire what the great masters succeeded so well in, namely, that power by which the chief objects, and even the minute finishing of parts, tell over everything that is meant to be subordinate in their pictures. Sir Joshua had this remarkably, and could even make the features of the face tell over everything, however strongly painted. I find that repose and breadth in the shadows and half-tints do a great deal towards it. Zoffany's figures derive great consequence from this; and I find that those who have studied light and shadow the most never appear to fail in it.

Wilkie.

XCV

The commonest error into which a critic can fall is the remark we so often hear that such-and-such an artist's work is "careless," and "would be better had more labour been spent upon it." As often as not this is wholly untrue. As soon as the spectator can see that "more labour has been spent upon it," he may be sure that the picture is to that extent incomplete and unfinished, while the look of freshness that is inseparable from a really successful picture would of necessity be absent. If the high finish of a picture is so apparent as immediately to force itself upon the spectator, he may know that it is not as it should be; and from the moment that the artist feels his work is becoming a labour, he may depend upon it it will be without freshness, and to that extent without the merit of a true work of art. Work should always look as though it had been done with ease, however elaborate; what we see should appear to have been done without effort, whatever may be the agonies beneath the surface. M. Meissonier surpasses all his predecessors, as well as all his contemporaries, in the quality of high finish, but what you see is evidently done easily and without labour. I remember Thackeray saying to me, concerning a certain chapter in one of his books that the critics agreed in accusing of carelessness; "Careless? If I've written that chapter once I've written it a dozen times--and each time worse than the last!" a proof that labour did not assist in his case. When an artist fails it is not so much from carelessness: to do his best is not only profitable to him, but a joy. But it is not given to every man--not, indeed, to any--to succeed whenever and however he tries. The best painter that ever lived never entirely succeeded more than four or five times; that is to say, no artist ever painted more than four or five masterpieces, however high his general average may have been, for such success depends on the coincidence, not only of genius and inspiration, but of health and mood and a hundred other mysterious contingencies. For my own part, I have often been laboured, but whatever I am I am never careless. I may honestly say that I never consciously placed an idle touch upon canvas, and that I have always been earnest and hard-working; yet the worst pictures I ever painted in my life are those into which I threw most trouble and labour, and I confess I should not grieve were half my works to go to the bottom of the Atlantic--if I might choose the half to go. Sometimes as I paint I may find my work becoming laborious; but as soon as I detect any evidence of that labour I paint the whole thing out without more ado.

Millais.

XCVI

I think that a work of art should not only be careful and sincere, but that the care and sincerity should also be evident. No ugly smears should be allowed to do duty for the swiftness which comes from long practice, or to find excuse in the necessity which the accomplished artist feels to speak distinctly. That necessity must never receive impulse from a desire to produce an effect on the walls of a gallery: there is much danger of this working unconsciously in the accomplished artist, consciously in the student.

Watts.

XCVII

Real effect is making out the parts. Why are we to be told that masters, who could think, had not the judgment to perform the inferior parts of art? (as Reynolds artfully calls them); that we are to learn to think from great masters, and to perform from underlings--to learn to design from Raphael, and to execute from Rubens?

Blake.

XCVIII

If I knew that my portrait was still at Antwerp, I would have it kept back for the case to be opened, so that one could see that it had not been hurt by so long a time spent in a case without being exposed to the air, and that, as often happens to colours freshly put on, it has not turned rather yellow, thereby losing all its first effect. The remedy, if this has happened, is to expose it repeatedly to the sun, the rays of which absorb the superfluity of oil which causes this change; and if at any time it still turns brown, it must be exposed afresh to the sun. Warmth is the only remedy for this serious mischief.

Rubens.

EFFECTS OF TIME ON PAINTING

XCIX

The only way to judge of the treasures the Old Masters of whatever age have left us--whether in architecture, sculpture, or painting--with any hope of sound deduction, is to look at the work and ask oneself--"What was that like when it was new?" The Elgin Marbles are allowed by common consent to be the perfection of art. But how much of our feeling of reverence is inspired by time? Imagine the Parthenon as it must have looked with the frieze of the mighty Phidias fresh from the chisel. Could one behold it in all its pristine beauty and splendour we should see a white marble building, blinding in the dazzling brightness of a southern sun, the figures of the exquisite frieze in all probability painted--there is more than a suspicion of that--and the whole standing out against the intense blue sky; and many of us, I venture to think, would cry at once, "How excessively crude." No; Time and Varnish are two of the greatest of Old Masters, and their merits and virtues are too often attributed by critics--I do not of course allude to the professional art-critics--to the painters of the pictures they have toned and mellowed. The great artists all painted in bright colours, such as it is the fashion nowadays for men to decry as crude and vulgar, never suspecting that what they applaud in those works is merely the result of what they condemn in their contemporaries. Take a case in point--the "Bacchus and Ariadne" in the National Gallery, with its splendid red robe and its rich brown grass. You may rest assured that the painter of that bright red robe never painted the grass brown. He saw the colour as it was, and painted it as it was--distinctly green; only it has faded with time to its present beautiful mellow colour. Yet many men nowadays will not have a picture with green in it; there are even buyers who, when giving a commission to an artist, will stipulate that the canvas shall contain none of it. But God Almighty has given us green, and you may depend upon it it's a fine colour.

Millais.

C

I must further dissent from any opinion that beauty of surface and what is technically called "quality" are mainly due to time. Sir John himself has quoted the early pictures of Rembrandt as examples of hard and careful painting, devoid of the charm and mystery so remarkable in his later work. The early works of Velasquez are still more remarkable instances, being, as they are, singularly tight and disagreeable--time having done little or nothing towards making them more agreeable.

Watts.

CI

I am painting for thirty years hence.

Monticelli.

CII

Sir John Millais is certainly right in his estimate of strong and even bright colour, but it seems to me that he is mistaken in believing that the colour of the Venetians was ever crude, or that time will ever turn white into colour. The colour of the best-preserved pictures by Titian shows a marked distinction between light flesh tones and white drapery. This is most distinctly seen in the small "Noli Me Tangere" in our National Gallery, in the so-called "Venus" of the Tribune and in the "Flora" of the Uffizi, both in Florence, and in Bronzino's "All is Vanity," also in the National Gallery. In the last-named picture, for example, the colour is as crude and the surface as bare of mystery as if it had been painted yesterday. As a matter of fact, white unquestionably tones down, but never becomes colour; indeed, under favourable conditions, and having due regard to what is underneath, it changes very little. In the "Noli Me Tangere" to which I have referred, the white sleeve of the Magdalen is still a beautiful white, quite different from the white of the fairest of Titian's flesh--proving that Titian never painted his flesh white.

The so-called "Venus" in the Tribune at Florence is a more important example still, as it is an elaborately painted picture owing nothing to the brightness that slight painting often has and retains, the colours being untormented by repeated re-touching. This picture is a proof that when the method is good and the pigments pure, the colours change very little. More than three hundred years have passed, and the white sheet on which the figure lies is still, in effect, white against the flesh. The flesh is most lovely in colour--neither violent by shadows or strong colour--but beautiful flesh. It cannot be compared to ivory or snow, or any other substance or material; it is simply beautiful lustre on the surface with a circulation of blood underneath--an absolute triumph never repeated except by Titian himself.

It is probable that the pictures by Reynolds are often lower in tone than they were, but it is doubtful whether the Strawberry Hill portraits are as much changed as may be supposed. Walpole, no doubt, called them "white and pinky," but it must be remembered that, living before the days of picture cleaning, he was accustomed to expect them to be brown and dark, probably even to associate colour with dirt in the Old Masters. The purer, clearer, and richer the colours are, the better a picture will be; and I think this should be especially insisted upon, since white is so effective in a modern exhibition that young artists are naturally prompted to profit by the means cheaply afforded and readily at hand.

I think it is probable that where Titian has used brown-green he intended it, since in many of the Venetian pictures we find green draperies of a beautiful colour. Sir John seems to infer that the colours used in the decoration of the Parthenon (no doubt used) were crude. The extraordinary refinements demonstrated in a lecture by Mr. Penrose on the spot last year, at which I had the good fortune to be present, forbid such a conclusion. A few graduated inches in the circumference of the columns, and deflection from straight line in the pediment and in the base-line, proved by measurement and examination to be carefully intentional, will not permit us for a moment to believe this could have been the case; so precise in line, rhythmical in arrangement, lovely in detail, and harmonious in effect, it could never have been crude in colour. No doubt the marble was white, but illuminated by such a sun, and set against such a sky and distance, the white, with its varieties of shadow, aided by the colours employed, could have gleaned life and flame in its splendour. Colour was certainly used, and the modern eye might at first have something to get over, but there could have been nothing harsh and crude. The exquisite purity of line and delicacy of edge could never have been matched with crudity or anything like harshness of colour. To this day the brightest colours may be seen on the columns at Luxor and Philae with beautiful effect.

Watts.

CIII

I am getting on with my pictures, and have now got them all three into a fairly forward state of under painting; completion, however, will only be reached in the course of next winter, for I intend to execute them with minute care. I have simplified my method of painting, and forsworn all tricks. I endeavour to advance from the beginning as much as possible, and equally try to mix the right tint, and slowly and carefully to put it on the right spot, and always with the model before me; what does not exactly suit has to be adapted; one can derive benefit from every head. Schwind says that he cannot work from models, they worry him! A splendid teacher for his pupils!

Nature worries every one at first, but one must so discipline oneself that, instead of checking and hindering, she shall illuminate and help, and solve all doubts. Has Schwind, with his splendid and varied gifts, ever been able to model a head with a brush? Those who place the brush behind the pencil, under the pretence that form is before all things, make a very great mistake. Form is certainly all-important; one cannot study it enough; but the greater part of form falls within the province of the tabooed brush. The ever-lasting hobby of contour which belongs to the drawing material is first the place where the form comes in; what, however, reveals true knowledge of form, is a powerful, organic, refined finish of modelling, full of feeling and knowledge--and that is the affair of the brush.

Leighton.

MANNER

CIV

Manner is always seductive. It is more or less an imitation of what has been done already, therefore always plausible. It promises the short road, the near cut to present fame and emolument, by availing ourselves of the labours of others. It leads to almost immediate reputation, because it is the wonder of the ignorant world. It is always accompanied by certain blandishments, showy and plausible, and which catch the eye. As manner comes by degrees, and is fostered by success in the world, flattery, &c., all painters who would be really great should be perpetually on their guard against it. Nothing but a close and continual observance of nature can protect them from the danger of becoming mannerists.

Constable.

CV

Have a holy horror of useless impasto, which gets sticky and dull, turns blue and heavy. When you have painted a bit of which you are doubtful, wait till the moment when it will be possible for you to take it out. Judge it; and if it is condemned, remove it firmly with your palette-knife, without rubbing by rags which spoil the limpidity of the pigment. You will have left a delicate foundation, to which you can return and finish with little labour, because your canvas will have received a first coating. Loading and massing the pigment is an abomination. In twenty-four hours gold turns to lead.

Puvis de Chavannes.

CVI

From the age of six I began to draw, and for eighty-four years I have worked independently of the schools, my thoughts all the time being turned towards drawing.

It being impossible to express everything in so small a space, I wished only to teach the difference between vermilion and crimson lake, between indigo and green, and also in a general way to teach how to handle round shapes and square, straight lines and curved; and if one day I make a sequel to this volume, I shall show children how to render the violence of ocean, the rush of rapids, the tranquillity of still pools, and among the living beings of the earth, their state of weakness or strength. There are in nature birds that do not fly high, flowering trees that never fruit; all these conditions of the life we live among are worth studying thoroughly; and if I ever succeed in convincing artists of this, I shall have been the first to show the way.

Hokusai.

CVII

Let every man who is here understand this well: design, which by another name is called drawing, and consists of it, is the fount and body of painting and sculpture and architecture and of every other kind of painting, and the root of all sciences. Let whoever may have attained to so much as to have the power of drawing know that he holds a great treasure; he will be able to make figures higher than any tower, either in colours or carved from the block, and he will not be able to find a wall or enclosure which does not appear circumscribed and small to his brave imagination. And he will be able to paint in fresco in the manner of old Italy, with all the mixtures and varieties of colour usually employed in it. He will be able to paint in oils very suavely with more knowledge, daring, and patience than painters. And finally, on a small piece of parchment he will be most perfect and great, as in all other manners of painting. Because great, very great is the power of design and drawing.

Michael Angelo.

DRAWING AND DESIGN

CVIII

Pupils, I give you the whole art of sculpture when I tell you--draw!

Donatello.

CIX

Drawing is the probity of art.

Ingres.

CX

To draw does not mean only to reproduce an outline, drawing does not consist only of line; drawing is more than this, it is expression, it is the inner form, the structure, the modelling. After that what is left? Drawing includes seven-eighths of what constitutes painting. If I had to put a sign above my door I would write on it "School of Drawing," and I am sure that I should turn out painters.

Ingres.

CXI

Draw with a pure but ample line. Purity and breadth, that is the secret of drawing, of art.

Ingres.

CXII

Continue to draw for long before you think of painting. When one builds on a solid foundation one can sleep at ease.

Ingres.

CXIII

The great painters like Raphael and Michael Angelo insisted on the outline when finishing their work. They went over it with a fine brush, and thus gave new animation to the contours; they impressed on their design force and fire.

Ingres.

CXIV

The first thing to seize in an object, in order to draw it, is the contrast of the principal lines. Before putting chalk to paper, get this well into the mind. In Girodet's work, for example, one sometimes sees this admirably shown, because through intense preoccupation with his model he has caught, willy-nilly, something of its natural grace; but it has been done as if by accident. He applied the principle without recognising it as such. X---- seems to me the only man who has understood it and carried it out. That is the whole secret of his drawing. The most difficult thing is to apply it, like him, to the whole body. Ingres has done it in details like hands, &c. Without mechanical aids to help the eye, it would be impossible to arrive at the principle; aids such as prolonging a line, &c., drawing often on a pane of glass. All the other painters, not excepting Michael Angelo and Raphael, draw by instinct, by inspiration, and found beauty by being struck with it in nature; but they did not know X----'s secret, accuracy of eye. It is not at the moment of carrying out a design that one ought to tie oneself down to working with measuring-rules, perpendiculars, &c.; this accuracy of eye must be an acquired habit, which in the presence of nature will spontaneously assist the imperious need of rendering her aspect. Wilkie, again, has the secret. In portraiture it is indispensable. When, for example, one has made out the ensemble of a design, and when one knows the lines by heart, so to speak, one should be able to reproduce them geometrically, in a fashion, on the picture. Above all with women's portraits; the first thing to seize is to seize the grace of the ensemble. If you begin with the details, you will be always heavy. For instance: if you have to draw a thoroughbred horse, if you let yourself go into details, your outline will never be salient enough.

Delacroix.

CXV

Drawing is the means employed by art to set down and imitate the light of nature. Everything in nature is manifested to us by means of light and its complementaries, reflection and shadow. This it is which drawing verifies. Drawing is the counterfeit light of art.

Bracquemond.

CXVI

It won't do to begin painting heads or much detail in this picture till it's all settled. I do so believe in getting in the bones of a picture properly first, then putting on the flesh and afterwards the skin, and then another skin; last of all combing its hair and sending it forth to the world. If you begin with the flesh and the skin and trust to getting the bones right afterwards, it's such a slippery process.

Burne-Jones.

CXVII

The creative spirit in descending into a pictorial conception must take upon itself organic structure. This great imaginative scheme forms the bony system of the work; lines take the place of nerves and arteries, and the whole is covered with the skin of colour.

Hsieh Ho (Chinese, sixth century).

CXVIII

Simplicity in composition or distinctness of parts is ever to be attended to, as it is one part of beauty, as has been already said: but that what I mean by distinctness of parts in this place may be better understood it will be proper to explain it by an example.

When you would compose an object of a great variety of parts, let several of those parts be distinguished by themselves, by their remarkable difference from the next adjoining, so as to make each of them, as it were, one well-shaped quantity or part (these are like what they call passages in music, and in writing paragraphs) by which means not only the whole, but even every part, will be better understood by the eye: for confusion will hereby be avoided when the object is seen near, and the shapes will seem well varied, though fewer in number, at a distance.

The parsley-leaf, in like manner, from whence a beautiful foliage in ornament was originally taken, is divided into three distinct passages; which are again divided into other odd numbers; and this method is observed, for the generality, in the leaves of all plants and flowers, the most simple of which are the trefoil and cinquefoil.

Observe the well-composed nosegay, how it loses all distinctness when it dies; each leaf and flower then shrivels and loses its distinct shape, and the firm colours fade into a kind of sameness; so that the whole gradually becomes a confused heap.

If the general parts of objects are preserved large at first, they will always admit of further enrichments of a small kind, but then they must be so small as not to confound the general masses or quantities; thus, you see, variety is a check upon itself when overdone, which of course begets what is called a petit taste and a confusion to the eye.

Hogarth.

CXIX

Drawing includes everything except the tinting of the picture.

Ingres.

CXX

One must always be drawing, drawing with the eye when one cannot draw with the pencil. If observation does not keep step with practice you will do nothing really good.

Ingres.

CXXI

As a means of practising this perspective of the variation and loss or diminution of the proper essence of colours, take at distances, a hundred braccia apart, objects standing in the landscape, such as trees, houses, men, and places, and in front of the first tree fix a piece of glass so that it is quite steady, and then let your eye rest upon it and trace out a tree upon the glass above the outline of the tree; and afterwards remove the glass so far to one side that the actual tree seems almost to touch the one that you have drawn. Then colour your drawing in such a way that the two are alike in colour and form, and that if you close one eye both seem painted on the glass and the same distance away. Then proceed in the same way with a second and a third tree, at distances of a hundred braccia from each other. And these will always serve as your standards and teachers when you are at work on pictures where they can be applied, and they will cause the work to be successful in its distance. But I find it is a rule that the second is reduced to four-fifths the size of the first when it is twenty braccia distant from it.

Leonardo.

CXXII

The great and golden rule of art, as well as of life, is this: That the more distinct, sharp, and wiry the bounding line, the more perfect the work of art.... Great inventors in all ages knew this: Protogenes and Apelles knew each other by this line; Raphael and Michael Angelo, and Albert Duerer, are known by this and this alone. The want of this determinate and bounding form evidences the idea of want in the artist's mind.

Blake.

CXXIII

My opinion is that he who knows how to draw well and merely does a foot or a hand or a neck, can paint everything created in the world; and yet there are painters who paint everything there is in the world so impatiently and so much without worth that it would be better not to do it at all. One recognises the knowledge of a great man in the fear with which he does a thing the more he understands it; and, on the contrary, the ignorance of others in the foolhardy daring with which they fill pictures with what they know nothing about. There may be an excellent master who has never painted more than a single figure, and without painting anything more deserves more renown and honour than those who have painted a thousand pictures: he knows better how to do what he has not done than the others know what they do.

Michael Angelo.

CXXIV

It is known that bodies in motion always describe some line or other in the air, as the whirling round of a firebrand apparently makes a circle, the waterfall part of a curve, the arrow and bullet, by the swiftness of their motions, nearly a straight line; waving lines are formed by the pleasing movement of a ship on the waves. Now, in order to obtain a just idea of action, at the same time to be judiciously satisfied of being in the right in what we do, let us begin with imagining a line formed in the air by any supposed point at the end of a limb or part that is moved, or made by the whole part or limb, or by the whole body together. And that thus much of movements may be conceived at once is evident, on the least recollection; for whoever has seen a fine Arabian war-horse, unbacked and at liberty, and in a wanton trot, cannot but remember what a large waving line his rising, and at the same time pressing forward cuts through the air, the equal continuation of which is varied by his curveting from side to side; whilst his long mane and tail play about in serpentine movements.

Hogarth.

CXXV

Distinguish the various planes of a picture by circumscribing them each in turn; class them in the order in which they present themselves to the daylight; before beginning to paint, settle which have the same value. Thus, for example, in a drawing on tinted paper make the parts that glitter gleam out with your white, then the lights, rendered also with white, but fainter; afterwards those of the half-tones that can be managed by means of the paper, then a first half-tone with the chalk, &c. When at the edge of a plane which you have accurately marked, you have a little more light than at the centre of it, you give so much more definition of its flatness or projection. This is the secret of modelling. It will be of no use to add black; that will not give the modelling. It follows that one can model with very slight materials.

Delacroix.

CXXVI

Take a style of silver or brass, or anything else provided the point is silver, sufficiently fine (sharp) and polished and good. Then to acquire command of hand in using the style, begin to draw with it from a copy as freely as you can, and so lightly that you can scarcely see what you have begun to do, deepening your strokes little by little, and going over them repeatedly to make the shadows. Where you would make it darkest go over it many times; and, on the contrary, make but few touches on the lights. And you must be guided by the light of the sun, and the light of your eye, and your hand; and without these three things you can do nothing properly. Contrive always when you draw that the light is softened, and that the sun strikes on your left hand; and in this manner you should begin to practise drawing only a short time every day, that you may not become vexed or weary.

Cennino Cennini.

CXXVII

Charcoal. You can't draw, you paint with it.

Pencil. It is always touch and go whether I can manage it even now. Sometimes knots will come in it, and I never can get them out--I mean little black specks. If I have once india-rubbered it, it doesn't make a good drawing. I look on a perfectly successful drawing as one built upon a groundwork of clear lines till it is finished. It's the same kind of thing with red chalk--it mustn't be taken out: rubbing with the finger is all right. In fact you don't succeed with any process until you find out how you may knock it about and in what way you must be careful. Slowly built-up texture in oil-painting gives you the best chance of changing without damage when it is necessary.

Burne-Jones.

CXXVIII

The simpler your lines and forms are the stronger and more beautiful they will be. Whenever you break up forms you weaken them. It is as with everything else that is split and divided.

Ingres.

CXXIX

The draperies with which you dress figures ought to have their folds so accommodated as to surround the parts they are intended to cover; that in the mass of light there be not any dark fold, and in the mass of shadows none receiving too great a light. They must go gently over, describing the parts; but not with lines across, cutting the members with hard notches, deeper than the part can possibly be; at the same time, it must fit the body, and not appear like an empty bundle of cloth; a fault of many painters, who, enamoured of the quantity and variety of folds, have encumbered their figures, forgetting the intention of clothes, which is to dress and surround the parts gracefully wherever they touch; and not to be filled with wind, like bladders puffed up where the parts project. I do not deny that we ought not to neglect introducing some handsome folds among these draperies, but it must be done with great judgment, and suited to the parts, where, by the actions of the limbs and position of the whole body, they gather together. Above all, be careful to vary the quality and quantity of your folds in compositions of many figures; so that, if some have large folds, produced by thick woollen cloth, others being dressed in thinner stuff, may have them narrower; some sharp and straight, others soft and undulating.

Leonardo.

CXXX

Do not spare yourself in drawing from the living model, draped as well as undraped; in fact, draw drapery continually, for remember that the beauty of your design must largely depend on the design of the drapery. What you should aim at is to get so familiar with all this that you can at last make your design with ease and something like certainty, without drawing from models in the first draught, though you should make studies from nature afterwards.

William Morris.

CXXXI

A woman's shape is best in repose, but the fine thing about a man is that he is such a splendid machine, so you can put him in motion, and make as many knobs and joints and muscles about him as you please.

Burne-Jones.

CXXXII

I want to draw from the nude this summer as much as I possibly can; I am sure that it is the only way to keep oneself up to the standard of draughtsmanship that is so absolutely necessary to any one who wishes to become a craftsman in preference to a glorified amateur.

C. W. Furse.

CXXXIII

Always when you draw make up your mind definitely as to what are the salient characteristics of the object, and express those as personally as you can, not minding whether your view is or is not shared by your relatives and friends. Now this is not carte blanche to be capricious, nor does it intend to make you seek for novelty; but if you are true to your own vision, as heretofore you have been, you will always be original and personal in your work. In stating your opinion on the structural character of man, bird, or beast, always wilfully caricature; it gives you something to prune, which is ever so much more satisfactory than having constantly to fill gaps which an unincisive vision has caused, and which will invariably make work dull and mediocre and wooden.

C. W. Furse.

CXXXIV

In Japanese painting form and colour are represented without any attempt at relief, but in European methods relief and illusion are sought for.

Hokusai.

CXXXV

It is indeed ridiculous that most of our people are disposed to regard Western paintings as a kind of Uki-ye. As I have repeatedly remarked, a painting which is not a faithful copy of nature has neither beauty nor is worthy of the name. What I mean to say is this: be the subject what it may, a landscape, a bird, a bullock, a tree, a stone, or an insect, it should be treated in a way so lifelike that it is instinct with life and motion. Now this is beyond the possibility of any other art save that of the West. Judged from this point of view, Japanese and Chinese paintings look very puerile, hardly deserving the name of art. Because people have been accustomed to such daub-like productions, whenever they see a master painting of the West, they merely pass it by as a mere curiosity, or dub it a Uki-ye, a misconception which betrays sheer ignorance.

Shiba Kokan (Japanese, eighteenth century).

CXXXVI

These accents are to painting what melody is to the harmonic base, and more than anything else they decide victory or defeat. A method is of little account at those moments when the final effect is at hand; one uses any means, even diabolical invocations, and when the need comes, when I have exhausted the resources of pigment, I use a scraper, pumice-stone, and if nothing else serves, the handle of my brush.

Rousseau.

CXXXVII

The noblest relievo in painting is that which is resultant from the treatment of the masses, not from the vulgar swelling and rounding of the bodies; and the noble Venetian massing is excellent in this quality. Those parts in which there is necessity for salient quality of relief must be expressed with a certain quadrature, a certain varied grace of accent like that which the bony ridge develops in beautiful wrists and ankles, also in some of the tunic-folds that fall behind the arm of the recumbent Fate over the middle of the figure of the Newlands Titian; and again in some of the happiest passages in the graceful women of Lodovico Caracci, and in their vesture folds, e.g. the bosom and waist of the St. Catherine.

Doubtless there is a choice, or design were vain. There must be courage to reject no less than to gather. A man is at liberty to neglect things that are repugnant to his disposition. He may, if he please, have nothing to do with thistle or thorn, with bramble or brier.... Nevertheless sharp and severe things are yet dear to some souls. Nor should I understand the taste that would reject the wildness of the thorn and holly, or the child-loving labyrinths of the bramble, or wholesome ranges of the downs and warrens fragrant with gorse.

No one requires of the painter that he even attempt to render the multitude and infinitude of Nature; but that he represent it through the chastened elements of his proper instrument, with a performance rendered distinctive and facile by study and genial impulse.

Edward Calvert.

CXXXVIII

Modelling is parent of the art of chasing, as of the art of sculpturing. Skilful as he was in these arts, he executed nothing which he had not modelled.

Pasiteles.

CXXXIX

Don't invent arrangements, select them, leaving out what you consider to be unimportant, and above all things don't be influenced in the arrangements you select by any pictures you may see, except perhaps the Japanese.

C. W. Furse.

CXXXIXa

He alone can conceive and compose who sees the whole at once before him.

Fuseli.

COLOUR

CXL

He who desires to be a painter must learn to rule the black, and red, and white.

Titian.

CXLI

There is the black which is old and the black which is fresh, lustrous black and dull black, black in sunlight and black in shadow. For the old black, one must use an admixture of red; for the fresh black, an admixture of blue; for the dull black, an admixture of white; for lustrous black, gum must be added; black in sunlight must have grey reflections.

Hokusai.

CXLII

When you are painting put a piece of black velvet between your eye and nature; by this means you will easily convince yourself that in nature everything is blond, even the dark trunks of trees relieved against the sky. Black, when it is in shadow, is strong in tone, but ceases to be black.

Dutilleux.

CXLIII

The Variation of Colour in uneven Superficies, is what confounds an unskilful

Painter; but if he takes Care to mark the Outlines of his Superficie, and the Seat of his Lights, he will find the true Colouring no such difficult matter: For first he will alter the Superficies properly as far as the Line of Separation, either with White or Black sparingly as only with gentle Dew; then he will in the same Manner bedew the other Side of the Line, if I may be allowed the expression, then this again and so on by turns, till the light Side is brightened with more transparent Colour, and the same Colour on the other Side dies away like Smoak into an easy Shade. But you should always remember, that no Superficie should ever be made so white that you cannot make it still brighter: Even in Painting the whitest Cloaths you should abstain from coming near the strongest of that Colour; because the Painter has nothing but White wherewith to imitate the Polish of the most shining Superficie whatsoever, as I know of none but Black with which he can represent the utmost Shade and Obscurity of Night. For this Reason, when he paints a white Habit, he should take one of the four Kinds of Colours that are clear and open; and so again in painting any black Habit, let him use another Extream, but not absolute Black, as for Instance, the Colour of the Sea where it is very deep, which is extreamly dark. In a Word, this Composition of Black and White has so much Power, that when practised with Art and Method, it is capable of representing in Painting the Superficie either of Gold or of Silver, and even of the clearest Glass. Those Painters, therefore, are greatly to be condemned, who make use of White immoderately and of Black without Judgment; for which reason I could wish that the Painters were obliged to buy their White at a greater Price than the most costly Gems, and that both White and Black were to be made of those Pearls which Cleopatra dissolved in Vinegar; that they might be more chary of it.

Leon Battista Alberti.

CXLIV

A word as to colour. One can only give warnings against possible faults; it is clearly impossible to teach colour by words, even ever so little of it, though it can be taught in a workshop, at least partially. Well, I should say, be rather restrained than over-luxurious in colour, or you weary the eye. Do not attempt over-refinements in colour, but be frank and simple. If you look at the pieces of colouring that most delight you in ornamental work, as, e.g. a Persian carpet, or an illuminated book of the Middle Ages, and analyse its elements, you will, if you are not used to the work, be surprised at the simplicity of it, the few tints used, the modesty of the tints, and therewithal the clearness and precision of all boundary lines. In all fine flat colouring there are regular systems of dividing colour from colour. Above all, don't attempt iridescent blendings of colour, which look like decomposition. They are about as much as possible the reverse of useful.

William Morris.

CXLV

After seeing all the fine pictures in France, Italy, and Germany, one must come to this conclusion--that colour, if not the first, is at least an essential quality in painting. No master has as yet maintained his ground beyond his own time without it. But in oil painting it is richness and depth alone that can do justice to the material. Upon this subject every prejudice with which I left home is, if anything, not only confirmed but increased. What Sir Joshua wrote, and what our friend Sir George so often supported, was right; and after seeing what I have seen, I am not now to be talked out of it.

With us, as you know, every young exhibitor with pink, white, and blue, thinks himself a colourist like Titian; than whom perhaps no painter is more misrepresented or misunderstood. I saw myself at Florence his famous Venus upon an easel, with Kirkup and Wallis by me. This picture, so often copied, and every copy a fresh mistake, is, what I expected it to be, deep yet brilliant; indescribable in its hues, yet simple beyond example in its execution and its colouring. Its flesh (O how our friends at home would stare!) is a simple, sober, mixed-up tint, and apparently, like your skies, completed while wet. No scratchings, no hatchings, no scumbling nor multiplicity of repetitions--no ultramarine lakes nor vermilions--not even a mark of the brush visible; all seemed melted in the fat and glowing mass, solid yet transparent, giving the nearest approach to life that the painter's art has ever yet reached.

Wilkie.

CXLVI

In painting, get the main tones first. Do not forget that white by itself should be used very sparingly; to make anything of a beautiful colour, accentuate the tones clearly, lay them fresh and in facets; no compromise with ambiguous and false tones; colour in nature is a mixture of single tones adapted to one another.

Chasseriau.

CXLVII

A thing to remember always: avoid greenish tones.

Chasseriau.

CXLVIII

One is a colourist by values, by colour and light; there are colourists who are luminarists as there are colourists pure and simple. Titian is a colourist but not a luminarist, while Correggio is a colourist and a luminarist.

The simple colourists are those who content themselves with representing the tones in their value and colour without troubling about the magic of light; they also give to tones all their intensity.

The luminarists, as the word indicates, make light the most important thing. Three names will make you understand; Rembrandt, Correggio, and Claude Lorraine.

Claude, taking the light of the sun for a starting-point, justifies his method by nature: you know that he starts from a luminous point, and that point is the sun. To make this brilliant you must make great sacrifices, for you have no doubt remarked that we painters always begin with a half-tint; as our paintings are not brightened by the light of the sun, and start with a half-tint, it is necessary by the magic of tones to make this half-tint shine like a luminous thing. You see that it is a difficult problem to solve; how does Claude do it? He does not copy the exact tones of nature, since beginning with a dull one, he is obliged to make it luminous. He transposes as in music; he observes all things constituting light, remarks that the rays prevent us from seizing the outline of a bright object, that then the flame is enveloped by a bright halo; then by a second one less vivid, and so on until the tones become dull and sombre. In short, to make myself understood, his picture seen from distance represents a flame.

Correggio also works in this way. Take for example his picture of Antiope.

The woman, enveloped in a panther skin, is as bright as a flame. The soft red tone forms the first halo, then the light blue draperies with a slight greenish tint form the second halo. The Satyr has a value a few degrees below that of the draperies, making it the third halo. When the bouquet is thus formed, Correggio surrounds it with beautiful dark leaves, shading towards the extremities of the canvas. These gradations are so well observed, that if you put the picture at so great a distance that you cannot see the figures, you will still have the representation of light.

Couture.

CXLIX

Painters who are not colourists make illuminations and not paintings. Painting, properly speaking--unless one wants to produce a monochrome--implies the idea of colour as one of its fundamental elements, together with chiaroscuro, proportion, and perspective. Proportion applies to sculpture as to painting. Perspective determines the outline; chiaroscuro produces relief by the arrangement of shadow and light in relation to the background; colour gives the appearance of life, &c.

The sculptor does not begin his work with an outline; he builds up with his material a likeness of the object which, rough at first, establishes from the beginning the essential conditions of relief and solidity.

Colourists, being those who unite all the qualities of painting, must, in a single process and at first setting to work, secure the conditions peculiar and essential to their art.

They have to mass with colour, as the sculptor with clay, marble, or stone; their sketch, like the sculptor's, must show proportion, perspective, effect, and colour.

Outline is as ideal and conventional in painting as in sculpture; it should result naturally from the good arrangement of the essential parts. The combined preparation of effect which implies perspective and colour will approach more or less the actual aspect of things, according to the degree of the painter's skill; but this foundation will contain potentially everything included in the final result.

Delacroix.

CL

I believe colour to be a quite indispensable quality in the highest art, and that no picture ever belonged to the highest order without it; while many, by possessing it--as the works of Titian--are raised certainly into the highest class, though not to the very highest grade of that class, in spite of the limited degree of their other great qualities. Perhaps the only exception which I should be inclined to admit exists in the works of Hogarth, to which I should never dare to assign any but the very highest place, though their colour is certainly not a prominent feature in them. I must add, however, that Hogarth's colour is seldom other than pleasing to myself, and that for my own part I should almost call him a colourist, though not aiming at colour. On the other hand, there are men who, merely on account of bad colour, prevent me from thoroughly enjoying their works, though full of other qualities. For instance, Wilkie or Delaroche (in nearly all his works, though the Hemicycle is fine in colour). From Wilkie I would at any time prefer a thoroughly fine engraving--though of course he is in no respect even within hail of Hogarth. Colour is the physiognomy of a picture; and, like the shape of the human forehead, it cannot be perfectly beautiful without proving goodness and greatness. Other qualities are in its life exercised; but this is the body of its life, by which we know and love it at first sight.

Rossetti.

CLI

In regard to the different modes of painting the flesh, I belief it is of little consequence which is pursued, if you only keep the colours distinct; too much mixing makes them muddy and destroys their brilliancy, you know. Sir Joshua was of opinion that the grey tints in the flesh of Titian's pictures were obtained by scumbling cool tints over warm ones; and others prefer commencing in a cool grey manner, and leaving the greys for the middle tints, whilst they paint upon the lights with warmer colours, also enriching the shadows with warmer and deeper colours too. But for my own part, I have always thought it a good way to consider the flesh as composed of different coloured network laid over each other, as is really the case in nature, and may be seen by those who will take the pains to look carefully into it.

Northcote.

CLII

The utmost beauty of colouring depends on the great principle of varying by all the means of varying, and on the proper and artful union of that variety.

I am apt to believe that the not knowing nature's artful and intricate method of uniting colours for the production of the variegated composition, or prime tint of flesh, hath made colouring, in the art of painting, a kind of mystery in all ages; insomuch, that it may fairly be said, out of the many thousands who have labour'd to attain it, not above ten or twelve painters have happily succeeded therein; Correggio (who lived in a country village, and had nothing but the life to study after) is said almost to have stood alone for this particular excellence. Guido, who made beauty his chief aim, was always at a loss about it. Poussin scarce ever obtained a glimpse of it, as is manifest by his many different attempts: indeed France hath not produced one remarkable good colourist.

Rubens boldly, and in a masterly manner, kept his bloom tints bright, separate, and distinct, but sometimes too much so for easel or cabinet pictures; however, his manner was admirably well calculated for great works, to be seen at a considerable distance, such as his celebrated ceiling at Whitehall Chapel: which upon a nearer view will illustrate what I have advanc'd with regard to the separate brightness of the tints; and shew, what indeed is known to every painter, that had the colours there seen so bright and separate been all smooth'd and absolutely blended together, they would have produced a dirty grey instead of flesh-colour. The difficulty then lies in bringing blue, the third original colour, into flesh, on account of the vast variety introduced thereby; and this omitted, all the difficulty ceases; and a common sign-painter that lays his colours smooth, instantly becomes, in point of colouring, a Rubens, a Titian, or a Correggio.

Hogarth.

CLIII

COPY ON CANVAS IN OIL OF THE DORIA CORREGGIO IN THE PALAZZO

PASQUA

It seems painted in (their) juicy, fat colour, the parts completed one after another upon the bare pannel, the same as frescoes upon the flattened wall. Simplicity of tint and of colour prevails; no staining or mottled varieties: the flesh, both in light and shadow, is produced by one mixed up tint so melted that no mark of the brush is seen. There is here no scratching or scumbling--no repetitions; all seems prepared at once for the glaze, which, simple as the painting is, gives to it with fearless hand the richness and glow of Correggio. All imitations of this master are complicated compared to this, and how complicated and abstruse does it make all attempts of the present day to give similar effects in colouring! Here is one figure in outline upon the prepared board, with even the finger-marks in colour of the painter himself. Here is the preparation of the figures painted up at once, and, strange to say, with solid and even sunny colours. Here are the heads of a woman and of a naked child, completed with the full zest and tone of Correggio, in texture fine, and in expression rich and luxurious, and as fine an example of his powers as any part to be found in his most celebrated work.

Wilkie.

CLIV

In a modern exhibition pictures lose by tone at first glance, but in the Louvre pictures gained, and Titian, Correggio, Rubens, Cuyp, and Rembrandt combated everything by the depth of their tones; and one still hopes that, when toning is successfully done, it will prevail.

You have now got your exhibition open in Edinburgh: do you find tone and depth an advantage there or not? Painting bright and raw, if one can find in his heart to lower and glaze it afterwards, is always satisfactory; but unless strength can be combined with this, it will never be the fashion in our days.

Wilkie.

CLV

I went into the National Gallery and refreshed myself with a look at the pictures. One impression I had was of how much more importance the tone of them is than the actual tint of any part of them. I looked close into the separate colours and they were all very lovely in their quality--but the whole colour-effect of a picture then is not very great. It is the entire result of the picture that is so wonderful. I peered into the whites to see how they were made, and it is astonishing how little white there would be in a white dress--none at all, in fact--and yet it looks white. I went again and looked at the Van Eyck, and saw how clearly the like of it is not to be done by me. But he had many advantages. For one thing, he had all his objects in front of him to paint from. A nice, clean, neat floor of fair boards well scoured, pretty little dogs and everything. Nothing to bother about but making good portraits--dresses and all else of exactly the right colour and shade of colour. But the tone of it is simply marvellous, and the beautiful colour each little object has, and the skill of it all. He permits himself extreme darkness though. It's all very well to say it's a purple dress--very dark brown is more the colour of it. And the black, no words can describe the blackness of it. But the like of it is not for me to do--can't be--not to be thought of.

As I walked about there I thought if I had my life all over again, what would I best like to do in the way of making a new start once more; it would be to try and paint more like the Italian painters. And that's rather happy for a man to feel in his last days--to find that he is still true to his first impulse, and doesn't think he has wasted his life in wrong directions.

Burne-Jones.

CLVI

All painting consists of sacrifices and parti-pris.

Goya.

CLVII

In nature, colour exists no more than line,--there is only light and shade. Give me a piece of charcoal, and I will paint your portrait for you.

Goya.

CLVIII

It requires much more observation and study to arrive at perfection in the shadowing of a picture than in merely drawing the lines of it. The proof of this is, that the lines may be traced upon a veil or a flat glass placed between the eye and the object to be imitated. But that cannot be of any use in shadowing, on account of the infinite gradation of shades, and the blending of them which does not allow of any precise termination; and most frequently they are confused, as will be demonstrated in another place.

Leonardo.

LIGHT AND SHADE

CLIX

Forget not therefore that the principal part of Painting or Drawing after the life consisteth in the truth of the line, as one sayeth in a place that he hath seen the picture of her Majesty in four lines very like, meaning by four lines but the plain lines, as he might as well have said in one line, but best in plain lines without shadowing; for the line without shadow showeth all to a good Judgement, but the shadow without line showeth nothing, as, for example, though the shadow of a man against a white wall sheweth like a man, yet it is not the shadow but the line of the shadow, which is so true that it resembleth excellently well, as drawn by that line about the shadow with a coal, and when the shadow is gone it will resemble better than before, and may, if it be a fair face, have sweet countenance even in the line; for the line only giveth the countenance, but both line and colour giveth the lively likeness, and shadows shew the roundness and the effect or Defect of the light wherein the picture was drawn. This makes me to remember the words also and reasoning of her Majesty when first I came in her highness' presence to draw, who after shewing me how she noted great difference of shadowing in the works and Diversity of Drawers of sundry nations, and that the Italians who had the name to be cunningest and to Draw best, shadowed not. Requiring of me the reason of it, seeing that best to shew oneself needeth no shadow of place but rather the open light, to which I granted, affirmed that shadows in pictures were indeed caused by the shadow of the place or coming in of the light at only one way into the place at some small or high window, which many workmen covet to work in for ease to their sight, and to give unto them a grosser line and a more apparent line to be deserved, and maketh the work imborse well and show very well afar off, which to Limning work needeth not, because it is to be viewed of necessity in hand near unto the Eye. Here her Majesty conceived the reason, and therefore chose her place to sit in for that purpose in the open alley of a goodly garden, where no tree was near nor any shadow at all, save that as the Heaven is lighter than the earth, so must that little shadow that was from the earth; this her Majesty's curious Demand hath greatly bettered my Judgement, besides divers other like questions in Art by her most excellent Majesty, which to speak or write of were fitter for some better clerk. This matter only of the light let me perfect that no wise man longer remain in Error of praising much shadows in pictures which are to be viewed in hand; great pictures high or far off Require hard shadows to become the better then nearer in story work better than pictures of the life; for beauty and good favour is like clear truth, which is not shadowed with the light nor made to be obscured, as a picture a little shadowed may be borne withal for the rounding of it, but so greatly smutted or Darkened as some use Disgrace it, and in like truth ill told, if a very well favoured woman show in a place where is great shadow, yet showeth she lovely not because of the shadow but because of her sweet favour consisting in the line or proportion, even that little which the light scarcely showeth greatly pleaseth, proving the

Desire to see more.

Nicholas Hilliard.

CLX

The lights cast from small windows also present a strong contrast of light and shadow, more especially if the chamber lit by them is large; and this is not good to use in painting.

Leonardo.

CLXI

When you are drawing from nature the light should be from the north, so that it may not vary; and if it is from the south keep the window covered with a curtain so that though the sun shine upon it all day long the light will undergo no change. The elevation of the light should be such that each body casts a shadow on the ground which is of the same length as its height.

Leonardo.

CLXII

Above all let the figures that you paint have sufficient light and from above, that is, all living persons whom you paint, for the people whom you see in the streets are all lighted from above; and I would have you know that you have no acquaintance so intimate but that if the light fell on him from below you would find it difficult to recognise him.

Leonardo.

CLXIII

If by accident it should happen, that when drawing or copying in chapels, or colouring in other unfavourable places, you cannot have the light on your left hand, or in your usual manner, be sure to give relief to your figures or design according to the arrangement of the windows which you find in these places, which have to give you light, and thus accommodating yourself to the light on which side soever it may be, give the proper lights and shadows. Or if it were to happen that the light should enter or shine right opposite or full in your face, make your lights and shades accordingly; or if the light should be favourable at a window larger than the others in the above-mentioned places, adopt always the best light, and try to understand and follow it carefully, because, wanting this, your work would be without relief, a foolish thing without mastery.

Cennino Cennini.

CLXIV

You have heard about Merlin's magic art; here in Venice you may see that of Titian, Giorgione, and all the others. In the Palazzo Barbarigo we went to the room which is said to have been Titian's studio for some time. The window faces the south, and the sun is shining on the floor by two o'clock. This made us think, whether you should not, after all, let the sun be there while you are painting. A temperate sunlight in the room makes the lights golden, and through the many, crossing, warm reflections the shadows get clearer and more transparent. But the difficulty is to know how to deal with such a shimmer; it is easier to paint with the light coming from the north. On the other hand, you see that the Venetians never tried to render in painting the impression of real, open sunlight. Their delicate sense of colour found a greater delight in looking at the fine fused tones and shades which are seen when the sunlight is only reflected under the clear blue sky and between the high palaces. Therefore, you often think that you see, for instance, groups of gondoliers on the Piazzetta in gay silvery notes, as in any painting by Paolo Veronese; and in the warm daylight in the great, gorgeous halls of the Palazzo Ducale there are still figures walking about in a colour as golden and fresh as if they were paintings by Titian.

E. Lundgren.

PORTRAITURE

CLXV

Painting the face of a pretty young girl is like carving a portrait in silver. There may be great elaboration, but no likeness will be forthcoming. It is better to put the elaboration into the young lady's clothes, and trust to a touch here and a stroke there to bring out her beauty as it really is.

Ku K'ai-Chih (Chinese, fourth century).

CLXVI

Portraiture may be great art. There is a sense, indeed, in which it is perhaps the greatest art of any. And portraiture involves expression. Quite true, but expression of what? Of a passion, an emotion, a mood? Certainly not. Paint a man or a woman with the damned "pleasing expression," or even the "charmingly spontaneous" so dear to the "photographic artist," and you see at once that the thing is a mask, as silly as the old tragic and comic mask. The only expression allowable in great portraiture is the expression of character and moral quality, not of anything temporary, fleeting, and accidental. Apart from portraiture you don't want even so much, or very seldom: in fact, you only want types, symbols, suggestions. The moment you give what people call expression, you destroy the typical character of heads and degrade them into portraits which stand for nothing.

Burne-Jones.

CLXVII

It produces a magnificent effect to place whole figures and groups, which are in shade, against a light field. The contrary, i.e. figures that are in light against a dark field, cannot be so perfectly expressed, because every illuminated figure, with or without a side light, will have some shade. The nearest approach to this is when the object so treated happen to be very fair, with other objects reflecting into their shades.

Shade against shade is indefinite. Light and shade against shade are mediate. Light against shade is perspicuous. Light and shade against light is mediate. Light against light is indefinite or indistinct.

Edward Calvert.

CLXVIII

Most of the masters have had a way, slavishly imitated by their schools and following, of exaggerating the darkness of the backgrounds which they give their portraits. They thought in this way to make the heads more interesting, but this darkness of background, in conjunction with faces lighted as we see them in nature, deprives these portraits of that character of simplicity which should be dominant in them. This darkness places the objects intended to be thrown into relief in quite abnormal conditions. Is it natural that a face seen in light should stand out against a really dark background--that is to say, one which receives no light? Ought not the light which falls on the figure to fall also on the wall, or the tapestry against which the figure stands? Unless it should happen that the face stands out against drapery of an extremely dark tone--but this condition is very rare, or against the entrance of a cavern or cellar entirely deprived of daylight--a circumstance still rarer--the method cannot but appear factitious.

The chief charm in a portrait is simplicity. I do not count among true portraits those in which the aim has been to idealise the features of a famous man when the painter has to reconstruct the face from traditional likenesses; there, invention rightly plays a part. True portraits are those painted from contemporaries. We like to see them on the canvas as we meet them in daily life, even though they should be persons of eminence and fame.

Delacroix.

CLXIX

Verestchagin says the old-fashioned way of setting a portrait-head against a dark ground is not only unnecessary, but being usually untrue when a person is seen by daylight, should be exploded as false and unreal. But it is certain a light garish background behind a painted head will not permit that head to have the importance it should have in reality, when the actual facts, solidity, movement, play of light and shadow, personal knowledge of the individual or his history, joined to the effects of different planes, distances, materials, &c., will combine to invest the reality with interests the most subtle and dexterous artistic contrivances cannot compete with, and which certainly the artist cannot with reason be asked to resign. A sense of the power of an autocrat, from whose lips one might be awaiting consignment to a dungeon or death, would be as much felt if he stood in front of the commonest wall-paper, in the commonest lodging-house, in the meanest watering-place, but no such impressions could be conveyed by the painter who depicted such surroundings. Lastly, I must strongly dissent from the opinion recently expressed by some, that seems to imply that a portrait-picture need have no interest excepting in the figure, and that the background had better be without any. This may be a good principle for producing an effect on the walls of an exhibition-room, where the surroundings are incongruous and inharmonious; an intellectual or beautiful face should be more interesting than any accessories the artist could put into the background. No amount of elaboration in the background could disturb the attention of any one looking at the portrait of Julius the Second by Raphael, also in the Tribune, which I cannot help thinking is the finished portrait in the world. A portrait is the most truly historical picture, and this the most monumental and historical of portraits. The longer one looks at it the more it demands attention. A superficial picture is like a superficial character--it may do for an acquaintance, but not for a friend. One never gets to the end of things to interest and admire in many old portrait-pictures.

Watts.

CLXX

There is one point that has always forced itself upon me strongly in comparing the portrait-painting qualities of Rembrandt and Velasquez. In Rembrandt I see a delightful human sympathy between himself and his sitters; he is always more interested in that part of them which conforms to some great central human type, and is comparatively uninterested in those little distinctions which delight the caricaturist and are the essence of that much applauded quality, "the catching of a likeness." I don't believe he was a very good catcher of likenesses, but I am sure his rendering was the biggest and fullest side of that man--there is always a fine ironical appreciation of character moulded by circumstance; whereas in Velasquez I find the other thing.

C. W. Furse.

CLXXI

I have wished to oblige the beholder, on looking at the portrait, to think wholly of the face in front of him, and nothing of the man who painted it. And it is my opinion that the artist who paints portraits in this way need have no fear of the pitfall of mannerism either in treatment or touch.

Watts.

CLXXII

Let us ... examine modern portraits. I shut my eyes and think of those full lengths in the New Gallery and the Academy, which I have not seen this year, but whose every detail is familiar to me. You will find that a uniform light stretches from their chins to their toes; in all probability the background is a slab of grey into whose insensitive surface neither light nor air penetrates; or perhaps that most offensive portrait-painter's property, a sham room in which none of the furniture has been seen in its proper relation of light to the face, but has been muzzed in with slippery insincerity, and with an amiable hope that it may take its place behind the figure. The face, in all but one or two portraits, will lack definition of plane--will be flat and flabby. A white spot on the nose and high light on the forehead will serve for modelling; little or no attempt will have been made to get a light which will help the observer to concentrate on the head, or give the head its full measure of rotundity--your eyes will wander aimlessly from cheek to chiffon, from glinting satin to the pattern on the floor, forgetful of the purpose of the portrait, and only arrested by some dab of pink or mauve, which will remind you that the artist is developing a somewhat irrelevant colour scheme.

  For solidity, for the realisation of the great constructive planes of things, for that element of sculpture which exists in all good painting, you will look in vain. I am sure that in an average Academy there are not three real attempts to get the values--that is, the inevitable relation of objects in light and shade that must exist under any circumstances--and not one attempt to contrive an artificial composition of light and shade which shall concentrate the attention of the spectator on the crucial point, and shall introduce these delightful effects of dark things against light and light against dark, which lend such richness and variety of tone and such vitality of construction to Titian, Rembrandt, and Reynolds. If we turn for a moment to the National Gallery and look at Gainsborough's "Baillie Family," or Reynolds' "Three Ladies decorating the Term of Hymen," we see at once the difference; in Gainsborough's case the group is in a mellow flood of light, there are no strong shadows on any of the faces, and none of the figures are used to cast shadows on other figures in the group; and yet as you look you see the whole light of the picture culminating in the central head of the mother, the sides and bottom of the picture fade off into artificial shadow, exquisitely used, without which that glorious light would have been dissipated over the picture, losing all its effectiveness and carrying power. See how finely he has understood the reticent tones of the man behind, and how admirably the loosely painted convention of landscape background is made to carry on the purely artificial arrangement of light and shade. In the Reynolds the shadowed figure on the left, and the shadows that flit across the skirts of the other two figures, and the fine relief of the dark trees, give a wonderful richness of design to a picture that is not in other respects of the highest interest.

C. W. Furse.

CLXXIII

Why have I not before now finished the miniature I promised to Mrs. Butts? I answer I have not till now in any degree pleased myself, and now I must entreat you to excuse faults, for portrait painting is the direct contrary to designing and historical painting in every respect. If you have not nature before you for every touch, you cannot paint portrait; and if you have nature before you at all, you cannot paint history. It was Michael Angelo's opinion and is mine.

Blake.

CLXXIV

I often find myself wondering why people are so frequently dissatisfied with their portraits, but I think I have discovered the principal reason--they are not pleased with themselves, and therefore cannot endure a faithful representation. I find it is the same with myself. I cannot bear any portraits of myself, except those of my own painting, where I have had the opportunity of coaxing them, so as to suit my own feelings.

Northcote.

LIGHT AND SHADE

CLXXV

Don't be afraid of splendour of effect; nothing is more brilliant, nothing more radiant than nature. Painting tends to become confused and to lose its power to strike hard. Make things monumental and yet real; set down the lights and the shadows as in reality. Heads which are all in a half-tone flushed with colour from a strong sun; heads in the light, full of air and freshness; these should be a delight to paint.

Chasseriau.

CLXXVI

The first object of a painter is to make a simple flat surface appear like a relievo, and some of its parts detached from the ground; he who excels all others in that part of the art deserves the greatest praise. This perfection of the art depends on the correct distribution of lights and shades called Chiaroscuro. If the painter, then, avoids shadows, he may be said to avoid the glory of the art, and to render his work despicable to real connoisseurs, for the sake of acquiring the esteem of vulgar and ignorant admirers of fine colours, who never have any knowledge of relievo.

Leonardo.

CLXXVII

Chiaroscuro, to use untechnical language and to speak of it as it is employed by all the schools, is the art of making atmosphere visible and painting objects in an envelope of air. Its aim is to create all the picturesque accidents of the shadows, of the half-tones and the light, of relief and distance, and to give in consequence more variety, more unity of effect, of caprice, and of relative truth, to forms as to colours. The opposite conception is one more ingenuous and abstract, a method by which one shows objects as they are, seen close, the atmosphere being suppressed, and in consequence without any perspective except the linear perspective, which results from the diminution in the size of objects and their relation to the horizon. When we talk of aeriel perspective we presuppose a certain amount of chiaroscuro.

Fromentin.

CLXXVIII

A painter must study his picture in every degree of light; it is all little enough. You know, I suppose, that this period of the day between daylight and darkness is called "the painter's hour"? There is, however, this inconvenience attending it, which allowance must be made for--the reds look darker than by day, indeed almost black, and the light blues turn white, or nearly so. This low, fading light also suggests many useful hints as to arrangement, from the circumstance of the dashings of the brush in a picture but newly commenced, suggesting forms that were not originally intended, but which often prove much finer ones. Ah, sometimes I see something very beautiful in these forms; but then I have such coaxing to do to get it fixed!--for when I draw near the canvas the vision is gone, and I have to go back and creep up to it again and again, and, at last, to hold my brush at the utmost length of my arm before I can fix it, so that I can avail myself of it the next day. The way to paint a really fine picture is first to paint it in the mind, to imagine it as strongly and distinctly as possible, and then to sketch it while the impression is strong and vivid.

I have frequently shut myself up in a dark room for hours, or even days, when I have been endeavouring to imagine a scene I was about to paint, and have never stirred till I had got it clear in my mind; then I have sketched it as quickly as I could, before the impression has left me.

Northcote.

DECORATIVE ART

CLXXIX

Decoration is the activity, the life of art, its justification, and its social utility.

Bracquemond.

CLXXX

The true function of painting is to animate wall-spaces. Apart from this, pictures should never be larger than one's hand.

Puvis de Chavannes.

CLXXXI

I want big things to do and vast spaces, and for common people to see them and say Oh!--only Oh!

Burne-Jones.

CLXXXII

I insist upon mural painting for three reasons--first, because it is an exercise of art which demands the absolute knowledge only to be obtained by honest study, the value of which no one can doubt, whatever branch of art the student might choose to follow afterwards; secondly, because the practice would bring out that gravity and nobility deficient in the English school, but not in the English character, and which being latent might therefore be brought out; and, thirdly, for the sake of action upon the public mind. For public improvement it is necessary that works of sterling but simple excellence should be scattered abroad as widely as possible. At present the public never see anything beautiful excepting in exhibition rooms, when the novelty of sight-seeing naturally disturbs the intellectual perceptions. It is a melancholy fact that scarcely a single object amongst those that surround us has any pretension to real beauty, or could be put simply into a picture with noble effect. And as I believe the love of beauty to be inherent in the human mind, it follows that there must be some unfortunate influence at work; to counteract this should be the object of a fine-art institution, and I feel assured if really good things were scattered amongst the people, it would not be long before satisfactory results exhibited themselves.

G. F. Watts.

CLXXXIII

I have ... gone for great masses of light and shade, relieved against one another, the only bright local colour being the blue of the workmens' coats and trousers. I have intentionally avoided the whole business of "flat decoration" by "making the things part of the walls," as one is told is so important. On the contrary, I have treated them as pictures and have tried to make holes in the wall--that is, as far as relief of strong light and shade goes; in the figures I have struggled to keep a certain quality of bas-relief--that is, I have avoided distant groups--and have woven my compositions as tightly as I can in the very foreground of the pictures, as without this I felt they would lose their weight and dignity, which does seem to me the essential business in a mural decoration, and which makes Puvis de Chavannes a great decorator far more than his flat mimicry of fresco does.... Tintoretto, in S. Rocco, is my idea of the big way to decorate a building; great clustered groups sculptured in light and shade filling with amazing ingenuity of design the architectural spaces at his disposal: a far richer and more satisfying result to me than the flat and unprofitable stuff which of late years has been called "decoration."...

Above all, I thoroughly disbelieve in the cant of mural decorations preserving the flatness of a wall. I see no merit in it whatever. Let them be massive as sculpture, but let every quality of value and colour lend them depth and vitality, and I am sure the hall or room will be richer and nobler as a result.

C. W. Furse.

CLXXXIV

People usually declare that landscape is an easy matter. I think it a very difficult one. For whenever you wish to produce a landscape, it is necessary to carry about the details, and work them out in the mind for some days before the brush may be applied. Just as in composition: there is a period of bitter thought over the theme; and until this is resolved, you are in the thrall of bonds and gyves. But when inspiration comes, you break loose and are free.

A Chinese Painter (about 1310 A.D.).

CLXXXV

One word: there are tendencies, and it is these which are meant by schools. Landscape, above all, cannot be considered from the point of view of a school. Of all artists the landscape painter is the one who is in most direct communion with nature, with nature's very soul.

Paul Huet.

CLXXXVI

From what motives springs the love of high-minded men for landscapes? In his very nature man loves to be in a garden with hills and streams, whose water makes cheerful music as it glides among the stones. What a delight does one derive from such sights as that of a fisherman engaging in his leisurely occupation in a sequestered nook, or of a woodman felling a tree in a secluded spot, or of mountain scenery with sporting monkeys and cranes!...

Though impatient to enjoy a life amidst the luxuries of nature, most people are debarred from indulging in such pleasures. To meet this want artists have endeavoured to represent landscapes so that people may be able to behold the grandeur of nature without stepping out of their houses. In this light, painting affords pleasures of a nobler sort by removing from one the impatient desire of actually observing nature.

Kuo Hsi (Chinese, eleventh century A.D.).

LANDSCAPE

CLXXXVII

Landscape is a big thing, and should be viewed from a distance in order to grasp the scheme of hill and stream. The figures of men and women are small matters, and may be spread out on the hand or on a table for examination, when they will be taken in at a glance. Those who study flower-painting take a single stalk and put it into a deep hole, and then examine it from above, thus seeing it from all points of view. Those who study bamboo-painting take a stalk of bamboo, and on a moonlight night project its shadow on to a piece of white silk on a wall; the true form of the bamboo is thus brought out. It is the same with landscape painting. The artist must place himself in communion with his hills and streams, and the secret of the scenery will be solved.... Hills without clouds look bare; without water they are wanting in fascination; without paths they are wanting in life; without trees they are dead; without depth-distance they are shallow; without level-distance they are near; and without height-distance they are low.

Kuo Hsi (Chinese, eleventh century A.D.).

CLXXXVIII

I have brushed up my "Cottage" into a pretty look, and my "Heath" is almost safe, but I must stand or fall by my "House." I had on Friday a long visit from

M---- alone; but my pictures do not come into his rules or whims of the art, and he said I had "lost my way." I told him that I had "perhaps other notions of art than picture admirers have in general. I looked on pictures as things to be avoided, connoisseurs looked on them as things to be imitated; and that, too, with such a deference and humbleness of submission, amounting to a total prostration of mind and original feeling; as must serve only to fill the world with abortions." But he was very agreeable, and I endured the visit, I trust, without the usual courtesies of life being violated.

What a sad thing it is that this lovely art is so wrested to its own destruction! Used only to blind our eyes, and to prevent us from seeing the sun shine, the fields bloom, the trees blossom, and from hearing the foliage rustle; while old--black--rubbed out and dirty canvases take the place of God's own works. I long to see you. I love to cope with you, like Jaques, in my "sullen moods," for I am not fit for the present world of art.... Lady Morley was here yesterday. On seeing the "House," she exclaimed, "How fresh, how dewy, how exhilarating!" I told her half of this, if I could think I deserved it, was worth all the talk and cant about pictures in the world.

Constable.

CLXXXIX

A wood all powdered with sunshine, all the tones of the trees illuminated and delicate, the whole in a mist of sun, and high lights only on the stems; a delicious, new, and rich effect.

Chasseriau.

CXC

The forests and their trees give superb strong tones in which violet predominates--above all, in the shadows--and give value to the green tones of the grass. The upright stems show bare with colours as of stones and of rocks--grey, tawny, flushed, always very luminous (like an agate) in the reflections: the whole takes a sombre colour which vies in vigour with the foreground.

A magnificent spectacle is that of mountains covered with ice and snow, towards evening, when the clouds roll up and hide their base. The summits may stand out in places against the sky. The blue background at such a time emphasises the warm gold colour of the shadows, and the lower parts are lost in a deep and sinister grey. We have seen this effect at Kandersteg.

Dutilleux.

CXCI

In your letter you wish me to give you my opinion of your picture. I should have liked it better if you had made it more of a whole--that is, the trees stronger, the sky running from them in shadow up to the opposite corner; that might have produced what, I think, it wanted, and have made it much less a two-picture effect.... I cannot let your sky go off without some observation. I think the character of your clouds too affected, that is, too much of some of our modern painters, who mistake some of our great masters; because they sometimes put in some of those round characters of clouds, they must do the same; but if you look at any of their skies, they either assist in the composition or make some figure in the picture--nay, sometimes play the first fiddle....

Breadth must be attended to if you paint; but a muscle, give it breadth. Your doing the same by the sky, making parts broad and of a good shape, that they may come in with your composition, forming one grand plan of light and shade--this must always please a good eye and keep the attention of the spectator, and give delight to every one.

Trifles in nature must be overlooked that we may have our feelings raised by seeing the whole picture at a glance, not knowing how or why we are so charmed. I have written you a long rigmarole story about giving dignity to whatever you paint--I fear so long that I should be scarcely able to understand what I mean myself. You will, I hope, take the will for the deed.

Old Crome.

CXCII

I am most anxious to get into my London painting-room, for I do not consider myself at work unless I am before a six-foot canvas. I have done a good deal of skying, for I am determined to conquer all difficulties, and that among the rest. And now, talking of skies, it is amusing to us to see how admirably you fight my battles; you certainly take the best possible ground for getting your friend out of a scrape (the example of the Old Masters). That landscape painter who does not make his skies a very material part of his composition neglects to avail himself of one of his greatest aids. Sir Joshua Reynolds, speaking of the landscapes of Titian, of Salvator, and of Claude, says: "Even their skies seem to sympathise with their subjects." I have often been advised to consider my sky as "a white sheet thrown behind the objects." Certainly, if the sky is obtrusive, as mine are, it is bad; but if it is evaded, as mine are not, it is worse; it must and always shall with me make an effectual part of the composition. It will be difficult to name a class of landscape in which the sky is not the keynote, the standard of scale, and the chief organ of sentiment. You may conceive, then, what a "white sheet" would do for me, impressed as I am with these notions, and they cannot be erroneous. The sky is the source of light in nature, and governs everything; even our common observations on the weather of every day are altogether suggested by it. The difficulty of skies in painting is very great, both as to composition and execution; because, with all their brilliancy, they ought not to come forward, or, indeed, be hardly thought of any more than extreme distances are; but this does not apply to phenomena or accidental effects of sky, because they always attract particularly. I may say all this to you, though you do not want to be told that I know very well what I am about, and that my skies have not been neglected, though they have often failed in execution, no doubt, from an over-anxiety about them which will alone destroy that easy appearance which nature always has in all her movements.

Constable.

CXCIII

He was looking at a seventy-four gun ship, which lay in the shadow under Saltash. The ship seemed one dark mass.

"I told you that would be the effect," said Turner, referring to some previous conversation. "Now, as you perceive, it is all shade!"

"Yes, I perceive it; and yet the ports are there."

"We can only take what is visible--no matter what may be there. There are people in the ship; we don't see them through the planks."

Turner.

CXCIV

Looked out for landscapes this evening; but although all around one is lovely, how little of it will work up into a picture! that is, without great additions and alterations, which is a work of too much time to suit my purpose just now. I want little subjects that will paint off at once. How despairing it is to view the loveliness of nature towards sunset, and know the impossibility of imitating it!--at least in a satisfactory manner, as one could do, would it only remain so long enough. Then one feels the want of a life's study, such as Turner devoted to landscape; and even then what a botch is any attempt to render it! What wonderful effects I have seen this evening in the hay-fields! The warmth of the uncut grass, the greeny greyness of the unmade hay in furrows or tufts with lovely violet shadows, and long shades of the trees thrown athwart all, and melting away one tint into another imperceptibly; and one moment more a cloud passes and all the magic is gone. Begin to-morrow morning, all is changed: the hay and the reapers are gone most likely; the sun too, or if not, it is in quite the opposite quarter, and all that was loveliest is all that is tamest now, alas! It is better to be a poet; still better a mere lover of Nature; one who never dreams of possession....

Ford Madox Brown.

CXCV

You should choose an old tumbledown wall and throw over it a piece of white silk. Then morning and evening you should gaze at it, until at length you can see the ruin through the silk--its prominences, its levels, its zigzags, and its cleavages, storing them up in the mind and fixing them in the eye. Make the prominences your mountains, the lower parts your water, the hollows your ravines, the cracks your streams, the lighter parts your nearer points, the darker parts your more distant points. Get all these thoroughly into you, and soon you will see men, birds, plants, and trees, flying and moving among them. You may then ply your brush according to your fancy, and the result will be of heaven, not of men.

Sung Ti (Chinese, eleventh century).

CXCVI

By looking attentively at old and smeared walls, or stones and veined marble of various colours, you may fancy that you see in them several compositions--landscapes, battles, figures in quick motion, strange countenances, and dresses, with an infinity of other objects. By these confused lines the inventive genius is excited to new exertions.

Leonardo.

CXCVII

Out by a quarter to eight to examine the river Brent at Hendon; a mere brooklet, running in most dainty sinuosity under overshadowing oaks and all manner of leafiness. Many beauties, and hard to choose amongst, for I had determined to make a little picture of it. However, Nature, that at first sight appears so lovely, is on consideration almost always incomplete; moreover, there is no painting intertangled foliage without losing half its beauties. If imitated exactly it can only be done as seen from one eye, and quite flat and confused therefore.

Ford Madox Brown.

CXCVIII

To gaze upon the clouds of autumn, a soaring exaltation in the soul; to feel the spring breeze stirring wild exultant thoughts;--what is there in the possession of gold and jewels to compare with delights like these? And then, to unroll the portfolio and spread the silk, and to transfer to it the glories of flood and fell, the green forest, the blowing winds, the white water of the rushing cascade, as with a turn of the hand a divine influence descends upon the scene. These are the joys of painting.

Wang Wei (Chinese, fifth century).

CXCIX

In the room where I am writing there are hanging up two beautiful small drawings by Cozens: one, a wood, close, and very solemn; the other, a view from Vesuvius looking over Portici--very lovely. I borrowed them from my neighbour, Mr. Woodburn. Cozens was all poetry, and your drawing is a lovely specimen.

Constable.

CXCIXa

Selection is the invention of the landscape painter.

Fuseli.

CC

Don't imagine that I do not like Corot's picture, La Prairie avec le fosse; on the contrary we thought, Rousseau and I, that it would be a pity to have one picture without the other, each makes so lively an impression of its own. You are perfectly right in liking the picture very much. What particularly struck us in the other one was that it has in an especial degree the look of being done by some one who knew nothing about painting but who had done his best, filled with a great longing to paint. In fact, a spontaneous discovery of the art! These are both very beautiful things. We will talk about them, for in writing one never gets to the end.

Millet.

CCI

TO ROUSSEAU

The day after I left you I went to see your exhibition.... To-day I assure you that in spite of knowing your studies of Auvergne and those earlier ones, I was struck once more in seeing them all together by the fact that a force is a force from its first beginnings.

With the very earliest you show a freshness of vision which leaves no doubt as to the pleasure you took in seeing nature, and one sees that she spoke directly to you, and that you saw her through your own eyes.

Your work is your own et non de l'aultruy, as Montaigne says. Don't think I mean to go through everything of yours bit by bit, down to the present moment. I only wish to mention the starting point, which is the important thing, because it shows that a man is born to his calling.

From the beginning you were the little oak which will grow into a big oak. There! I must tell you once more how much it moved me to see all this.

Millet.

CCII

I don't know if Corot is not greater than Delacroix. Corot is the father of modern landscape. There is no landscape painter of to-day who--knowingly or not--does not derive from him. I have never seen a picture of Corot's which was not beautiful, or a line which did not mean something.

Among modern painters it is Corot who as a colourist has most in common with Rembrandt. The colour scheme is golden with the one and grey with the other throughout the whole harmony of tones. In appearance their methods are the opposite of each other, but the desired result is the same. In a portrait by Rembrandt all details melt into shadow in order that the spectator's gaze may be concentrated on a single part, often the eyes, and this part is handled more caressingly than the rest.

Corot, on the other hand, sacrifices the details which are in the light--the extremities of trees, and so on--and brings us always to the spot which he has chosen for his main appeal to the spectator's eye.

Dutilleux.

CCIII

Landscape has taken refuge in the theatre; scene-painters alone understand its true character and can put it into practice with a happy result. But Corot?

Oh that man's soul rebounds like a steel spring; he is no mere landscape painter, but an artist--a real artist, and rare and exceptional genius.

Delacroix.

CCIV

TO VERWEE

There is an International Exhibition at Petit's now, and I am showing some sea-pieces there with great success. The exhibition is made up, with one or two exceptions, of young men. They are very clever, but all alike; they follow a fashion--there is no more individuality. Everybody paints, everybody is clever.

We shall end by adoring J. Dupre. I don't always like him, but he has individuality.

Too many painters, my dear fellow, and too many exhibitions! But you see, at my age, I'm not afraid of showing my pictures among the young men's sometimes.

Yet I hate exhibitions; one can hardly ever judge of a picture there.

Alfred Stevens.

ITALIAN MASTERS

CCV

There is something ... in those deities of intellect in the Sistine Chapel that converts the noblest personages of Raphael's drama into the audience of Michael Angelo, before whom you know that, equally with yourself, they would stand silent and awe-struck.

Lawrence.

CCVI

My only disagreement with you would be in the estimate of his comparative excellence in sculpture and painting. He called himself sculptor, but we seldom gauge rightly our own strength and weakness. The paintings in the Sistine Chapel are to my mind entirely beyond criticism or praise, not merely with reference to design and execution, but also for colour, right noble and perfect in their place. I was never more surprised than by this quality, to which I do not think justice has ever been done; nothing in his sculpture comes near to the perfection of his Adam or the majesty of the Dividing the Light from Darkness; his sculpture lacks the serene strength that is found in the Adam and many other figures in the great frescoes. Dominated by the fierce spirit of Dante, he was less influenced by the grave dignity of the Greek philosophy and art than might have been expected from the contemporary and possible pupil of Poliziano. In my estimate of him as a Sculptor in comparison with him as Painter, I am likely to be in a minority of one! but I think that when he is thought of as a painter his earlier pictures are thought of, and these certainly are unworthy of him, but the Prophets and Sibyls are the greatest things ever painted. As a rule he certainly insists too much upon the anatomy; some one said admirably, "Learn anatomy, and forget it"; Michael Angelo did the first and not the second, and the fault of almost all his work is, that it is too much an anatomical essay. The David is an example of this, besides being very faulty in proportion, with hands and feet that are monstrous. It Is, I think, altogether bad. The hesitating pose is good, and goes with the sullen expression of the face, but is not that of the ardent heroic boy!

This seems presumptuous criticism; and you might, considering my aspirations and efforts, say to me: "Do better!" but I am not Michael Angelo, but I am a pupil of the greatest sculptor of all, Pheidias (a master the great Florentine knew nothing of), and, so far, feel a right to set up judgment on the technique only.

Watts.

CCVII

ITALIAN ART IN FLANDERS

As to Italian art, here at Brussels there is nothing but a reminiscence of it. It is an art which has been falsified by those who have tried to acclimatise it, and even the specimens of it which have passed into Flanders lose by their new surroundings. When in a part of the gallery which is least Flemish, one sees two portraits by Tintoret, not of the first rank, sadly retouched, but typical--one finds it difficult to understand them side by side with Memling, Martin de Vos, Van Orley, Rubens, Van Dyck, and even Antonio More. It is the same with Veronese. He is out of his element; his colour is lifeless, it smacks of the tempera painter; his style seems frigid, his magnificence unspontaneous and almost bombastic. Yet the picture is a superb piece, in his finest manner; a fragment of an allegorical triumph taken from a ceiling in the Ducal Palace, and one of his best; but Rubens is close by, and that is enough to give the Rubens of Venice an accent which is not of this country. Which of the two is right? And listening merely to the language so admirably spoken by the two men, who shall decide between the correct and learned rhetoric of Venetian speech, and the emphatic, warmly coloured, grandiose incorrectness of the Antwerp idiom? At Venice one leans to Veronese; in Flanders one has a better ear for Rubens.

Italian art has this in common with all powerful traditions, that it is at the same time very cosmopolitan because it has penetrated everywhere, and very lofty because it has been self-sufficient. It is at home, in all Europe, except in two countries; Belgium, the genius of which it has appreciably affected without ever dominating it; and Holland, which once made a show of consulting it but which has ended by passing it by; so that, while it is on neighbourly terms with Spain, while it is enthroned in France, where, at least in historical painting, our best painters have been Romans, it encounters in Flanders two or three men, great men of a great race, sprung from the soil, who hold sway there and have no mind to share their empire with any other.

Fromentin.

CCVIII

I am never tired of looking at Titian's pictures; they possess such extreme breadth, which to me is so delightful a quality. In my opinion there never will, to the end of time, arise a portrait-painter superior to Titian. Next to him in this kind of excellence is Raphael. There is this difference between Raphael and Titian: Raphael, with all his excellence, possessed the utmost gentleness; it was as if he had said, "If another person can do better, I have no objections." But Titian was a man who would keep down every one else to the uttermost; he was determined that the art should come in and go out with himself; the expression in all the portraits of him told as much. When any stupendous work of antiquity remains with us--say, a building or a bridge--the common people cannot account for it, and they say it was erected by the devil. Now I feel this same thing in regard to the works of Titian;--they seem to me as if painted by a devil, or at any rate from inspiration; I cannot account for them.

Northcote.

NORTHERN MASTERS

CCIX

Raphael, to be plain with you--for I like to be candid and outspoken--does not please me at all. In Venice are found the good and the beautiful; to their brush I give the first place; it is Titian that bears the banner.

Velasquez.

CCX

Perhaps some day the world will discover that Rembrandt is a much greater painter than Raphael. I write this blasphemy--one to make the hair of the Classicists stand on end--without definitely taking a side; only I seem to find as I grow older that the most beautiful and most rare thing in the world is truth.

Let us say, if you will, that Rembrandt has not Raphael's nobility. Yet perhaps this nobility which Raphael manifests in his line is shown by Rembrandt in the mysterious conception of his subjects, in the profound naivete of his expressions and gestures. However much one may prefer the majestic emphasis of Raphael, which answers perhaps to the grandeur inherent in certain subjects, one might assert, without being stoned by men of taste--I mean men whose taste is real and sincere--that the great Dutchman was more a born painter than the studious pupil of Perugino.

Delacroix.

CCXI

Rembrandt's principle was to extract from things one element among the rest, or rather to abstract every element in order to concentrate on the seizure of one only. Thus in all his works he has set himself to analyse, to distil; or, in better phrase, has been metaphysician even more than poet. Reality never appealed to him by its general effects. One might doubt, from his way of treating human forms, whether their "envelope" interested him. He loved women, and never saw them otherwise than unshapely; he loved textures, and did not imitate them; but then, if he ignored grace and beauty, purity of line and the delicacy of the skin, he expressed the nude body by suggestions of suppleness, roundness, elasticity, with a love of material substance, a sense of the live being, which enchant the practical painter. He resolved everything into its component parts, colour as well as light, so that, by eliminating the complicated and condensing the scattered elements from a given scene, he succeeded in drawing without outline, in painting a portrait almost without strokes that show, in colouring without colour, in concentrating the light of the solar system into a sunbeam. It would be impossible in a plastic art to carry the curiosity for the essential to an intenser pitch. For physical beauty he substitutes expression of character; for the imitation of things, their almost complete transformation; for studious scrutiny, the speculation of the psychologist; for precise observation, whether trained or natural, the visions of a seer and apparitions of such vividness that he himself is deceived by them. By virtue of this faculty of second sight, of intuitions like those of a somnambulist, he sees farther into the supernatural world than any one else whatever. The life that he perceives in dream has a certain accent of the other world, which makes real life seem pale and almost cold. Look at his "Portrait of a Woman in the Louvre," two paces from "Titian's Mistress." Compare the two women, study closely the two pictures, and you will understand the difference between the two brains. Rembrandt's ideal, sought as in a dream with closed eyes, is Light: the nimbus around objects, the phosphorescence that comes against a black background. It is something fugitive and uncertain, formed of lineaments scarce perceptible, ready to disappear before the eye has fixed them, ephemeral and dazzling. To arrest the vision, to set it on the canvas, to give it its shape and moulding, to preserve the fragility of its texture, to render its brilliance, and yet achieve in the result a solid, masculine, substantial painting, real beyond any other master's work, and able to hold its own with a Rubens, a Titian, a Veronese, a Giorgione, a Van Dyck--this is Rembrandt's aim. Has he succeeded? The testimony of the world answers for him.

Fromentin.

CCXII

The painting of Flanders will generally satisfy any devout person more than the painting of Italy, which will never cause him to shed many tears; this is not owing to the vigour and goodness of that painting, but to the goodness of such devout person; women will like it, especially very old ones or very young ones. It will please likewise friars and nuns, and also some noble persons who have no ear for true harmony. They paint in Flanders, only to deceive the external eye, things that gladden you and of which you cannot speak ill, and saints and prophets. Their painting is of stuffs--bricks and mortar, the grass of the fields, the shadows of trees, and bridges and rivers, which they call landscapes, and little figures here and there; and all this, although it may appear good to some eyes, is in truth done without reasonableness or art, without symmetry or proportion, without care in selecting or rejecting, and finally, without any substance or verve; and in spite of all this, painting in some other parts is worse than it is in Flanders. Neither do I speak so badly of Flemish painting because it is all bad, but because it tries to do so many things at once (each of which alone would suffice for a great work), so that it does not do anything really well.

Only works which are done in Italy can be called true painting, and therefore we call good painting Italian; for if it were done so well in another country, we should give it the name of that country or province. As for the good painting of this country, there is nothing more noble or devout; for with wise persons nothing causes devotion to be remembered, or to arise, more than the difficulty of the perfection which unites itself with and joins God; because good painting is nothing else but a copy of the perfections of God and a reminder of His painting. Finally, good painting is a music and a melody which intellect only can appreciate, and with great difficulty. This painting is so rare that few are capable of doing or attaining to it.

Michael Angelo.

CCXIII

All Dutch painting is concave: what I mean is that it is composed of curves described about a point determined by the pictorial interest; circular shadows round a dominant light. Design, colouring, and lighting fall into a concave scheme, with a strongly defined base, a retreating ceiling, and corners rounded and converging on the centre; whence it follows that the painting is all depth, and that it is far from the eye to the objects represented. No type of painting leads with more certain directness from the foreground to the background, from the frame to the horizon. One can live in it, walk in it, see to the uttermost ends of it; one is tempted to raise one's head to measure the distance of the sky. Everything conspires to this illusion: the exactness of the aerial perspective, the perfect harmony of colour and tones with the plane on which the object is placed. The rendering of the heights of space, of the envelope of atmosphere, of the distant effect, which absorbs this school makes the painting of all other schools seem flat, something laid upon the surface of the canvas.

Fromentin.

CCXIV

In Van Eyck there is more structure, more muscle, more blood in the veins; hence the impressive virility of his faces and the strong style of his pictures. Altogether he is a portrait-painter of Holbein's kin--exact, shrewd, and with a gift of penetration that is almost cruel. He sees things with more perfect rightness than Memling, and also in a bigger and some summary way. The sensations which the aspect of things evokes in him are more powerful; his feeling for their colour is more intense; his palette has a fullness, a richness, a distinctness, which Memling's has not. His colour schemes are of more even power, better held together, composed of values more cunningly found. His whites are fatter, his purple richer, and the indigo blue--that fine blue as of old Japanese enamel, which is peculiar to him--has more depth of dye, more solidity of texture. The splendour and the costliness of the precious things, of which the superb fashions of his time were so lavish, appealed to him more strongly.

Fromentin.

CCXV

Van Eyck saw with his eyes, Memling begins to see with his soul. The one had a good and a right vein of thought; the other does not seem to think so much, but he has a heart which beats in a quite different way. The one copied and imitated, the other copies too and imitates, but transfigures. The former reproduced--without any preoccupation with the ideal types of humanity--above all, the masculine types, which passed before his eyes in every rank of the society of his time; the latter contemplates nature in a reverie, translates her with imagination, dwells upon everything which is most delicate and lovely in human forms, and creates, above all, in his type of woman a being exquisite and elect, unknown before and lost with him.

Fromentin

CCXVI

BRUGES, 1849

This is a most stunning place, immeasurably the best we have come to. There is a quantity of first-rate architecture, and very little or no Rubens.

But by far the best of all are the miraculous works of Memling and Van Eyck. The former is here in a strength that quite stunned us--and perhaps proves himself to have been a greater man even than the latter. In fact, he was certainly so intellectually, and quite equal in mechanical power. His greatest production is a large triptych in the Hospital of St. John, representing in its three compartments: firstly, the "Decollation of St. John Baptist"; secondly, the "Mystic Marriage of St. Catherine to the Infant Saviour"; and thirdly, the "Vision of St. John Evangelist in Patmos." I shall not attempt any description; I assure you that the perfection of character and even drawing, the astounding finish, the glory of colour, and, above all, the pure religious sentiment and ecstatic poetry of these works is not to be conceived or described. Even in seeing them the mind is at first bewildered by such godlike completeness; and only after some while has elapsed can at all analyse the causes of its awe and admiration; and then finds these feelings so much increased by analysis that the last impression left is mainly one of utter shame at its own inferiority.

Van Eyck's picture at the Gallery may give you some idea of the style adopted by Memling in these great pictures; but the effect of light and colour is much less poetical in Van Eyck's; partly owing to his being a more sober subject and an interior, but partly also, I believe, to the intrinsic superiority of Memling's intellect. In the background of the first compartment there is a landscape more perfect in the abstract lofty feeling of nature than anything I have ever seen. The visions of the third compartment are wonderfully mystic and poetical.

Rossetti.

CCXVII

VAN DYCK

Van Dyck completed Rubens by adding to his achievement portraits absolutely worthy of his master's brush, better than Rubens' own. He created in his own country an art which was original, and consequently he has his share in the creation of a new art. Besides this he did yet more: he begot a whole school in a foreign country, the English school--Reynolds, Lawrence, Gainsborough, and I would add to them nearly all the genre painters who are faithful to the English tradition, and the most powerful landscape painters issue directly from Van Dyck, and indirectly from Rubens through Van Dyck. These are high claims. And so posterity, always just in its instincts, gives Van Dyck a place apart between the men of the first and those of the second rank. The world has never decided the exact precedence which ought to be his in the procession of the masters, and since his death, as during his life, he seems to have held the privilege of being placed near the throne and of making a stately figure there.

Fromentin.

SPANISH PAINTING

CCXVIII

VELASQUEZ

What we are all trying to do with great labour, he does at once.

Reynolds.

CCXIX

Saw again to-day the Spanish school in the Museum,--Velasquez, a surprising fellow! The "Hermits in a Rocky Desert" pleased me much; also a "Dark Wood at Nightfall." He is Teniers on a large scale: his handling is of the most sparkling kind, owing much of its dazzling effect to the flatness of the ground it is placed upon.

The picture of "Children in Grotesque Dresses," in his painting-room, is a surprising piece of handling. Still he would gain, and indeed does gain, when he glazes his pictures. He makes no use of his ground; lights and shadows are opaque. Chilliness and blackness are sometimes the result; and often a cold blue or green prevails, requiring all his brilliancy of touch and truth of effect to make tolerable. Velasquez, however, may be said to be the origin of what is now doing in England. His feeling they have caught almost without seeing his works; which here seem to anticipate Reynolds, Romney, Raeburn, Jackson, and even Sir Thomas Lawrence. Perhaps there is this difference: he does at once what we do by repeated and repeated touches.

It may truly be said, that wheresoever Velasquez is admired, the paintings of England must be acknowledged and admired with him.

Wilkie.

CCXX

VELASQUEZ

Never did any one think less of a style or attain it more consummately. He was far too much occupied with the divining of the qualities of light and atmosphere that enveloped his subjects, and with stating those truths in the most direct and poignant way to have time to spare on mere adornments and artifices that amuse us in the work of lesser men. Every stroke in Velasquez means something, records an observation. You never see a splodge of light that entertains you for a moment and relapses into chic as you analyse it; even the most elusive bits of painting like the sword-hilt in the "Admiral Pulido" are utterly just, and observed as the light flickers and is lost over the steel shapes. No one ever had the faculty of observing the true character of two diverse forms at the same time as he did. If you look at any quilted sleeve you will feel the whole texture of the material and recognise its own shape, and yet under it and through it each nuance of muscle and arm-form reveals itself. It is no light praise, mind you, when one says that every touch is the record of a tireless observation--you have only to look at a great Sir Joshua to see that quite half of every canvas is merely a recipe, a painted yawn in fact, as the intensity of his vision relaxed; but in a Velasquez your attention is riveted by the passionate search of the master and his ceaseless absorption in the thing before him--and this is all the more astounding because the work is hardly ever conceived from a point of view of bravura; there is nothing over-enthusiastic, insincerely impetuous, but a quiet suave dignity informing the whole, and penetrating into the least detail of the canvas.

There is one quality Velasquez never falters in; from earliest days he is master of his medium; he understands its every limitation, realises exactly how far his palette is capable of rendering nature; and so you are never disturbed in your appreciation of his pictures by a sense that he is battling against insuperable difficulties, severely handicapped by an unsympathetic medium; but rather that here is the consummate workman who, gladly recognising the measure of his freedom within the four walls of his limitations, illustrates for you that fine old statement, "Whose service is perfect freedom."

C. W. Furse.

CCXXI

ON GAINSBOROUGH

We must not forget, whilst we are on this subject, to make some remarks on his custom of painting by night, which confirms what I have already mentioned,--his great affection to his art; since he could not amuse himself in the evening by any other means so agreeable to himself. I am indeed much inclined to believe that it is a practice very advantageous and improving to an artist: for by this means he will acquire a new and a higher perception of what is great and beautiful in nature. By candlelight not only objects appear more beautiful, but from their being in a greater breadth of light and shadow, as well as having a greater breadth and uniformity of colour, nature appears in a higher style; and even the flesh seems to take a higher and richer tone of colour. Judgment is to direct us in the use to be made of this method of study; but the method itself is, I am very sure, advantageous. I have often imagined that the two great colourists, Titian and Correggio, though I do not know that they painted by night, formed their high ideas of colouring from the effects of objects by this artificial light.

Reynolds.

MODERN PAINTING

CCXXII

ON REYNOLDS

Damn him! how various he is!

Gainsborough.

CCXXIII

I shall take advantage of Sir John's[3] mention of Reynolds and Gainsborough to provoke some useful refutation, by stating that it seems to me the latter is by no means the rival of the former; though in this opinion I should expect to find myself in a minority of one. Reynolds knew little about the human structure, Gainsborough nothing at all; Reynolds was not remarkable for good drawing, Gainsborough was remarkable for bad; nor did the latter ever approach Reynolds in dignity, colour, or force of character, as in the portraits of John Hunter and General Heathfield for example. It may be conceded that more refinement, and perhaps more individuality, is to be found in Gainsborough, but his manner (and both were mannerists) was scratchy and thin, while that of Reynolds was manly and rich. Neither Reynolds nor Gainsborough was capable of anything ideal; but the work of Reynolds indicates thought and reading, and I do not know of anything by Gainsborough conveying a like suggestion.

Watts.

[Footnote 3: Sir John Millais.]

CCXXIV

I was thinking yesterday, as I got up, about the special charm of the English school. The little I saw of it has left me memories. They have a real sensitiveness which triumphs over all the studies in concoction which appear here and there, as in our dismal school; with us that sensitiveness is the rarest thing: everything has the look of being painted with clumsy tools, and what is worse, by obtuse and vulgar minds. Take away Meissonier, Decamps, one or two others, and some of the youthful pictures of Ingres, and all is tame, nerveless, without intention, without fire. One need only cast one's eye over that stupid, commonplace paper L'Illustration, manufactured by pettifogging artists over here, and compare it with the corresponding English publication to realise how wretchedly flat, flabby, and insipid is the character of most of our productions. This supposed home of drawing shows really no trace of it, and our most pretentious pictures show as little as any. In these little English designs nearly every object is treated with the amount of interest it demands; landscapes, sea-pieces, costumes, incidents of war, all these are delightful, done with just the right touch, and, above all, well drawn.... I do not see among us any one to be compared with Leslie, Grant, and all those who derive partly from Wilkie and partly from Hogarth, with a little of the suppleness and ease introduced by the school of forty years back, Lawrence and his comrades, who shone by their elegance and lightness.

Delacroix.

CCXXV

THE ENGLISH SCHOOL

I shall never care to see London again. I should not find there my old memories, and, above all, I should not find the same men to enjoy with me what there is to be seen now. Perhaps I might find myself obliged to break a lance for Reynolds, or for that adorable Gainsborough, whom you are indeed right to love. Not that I am the opponent of the present movement in the painting of England. I am even struck by the prodigious conscientiousness that these people can bring to bear even on work of the imagination; it seems that in coming back to excessive detail they are more in their own element than when they imitated the Italian painters and the Flemish colourists. But what does the skin matter? Under this seeming transformation they are always English. Thus instead of making imitations pure and simple of the primitive Italians, as the fashion has been among us, they mix with this imitation of the manner of the old schools an infinitely personal sentiment; they put into it the interest which is generally missing in our cold imitations of the formulas and the style of schools which have had their day. I am writing without pulling myself up, and saying everything that comes into my head. Perhaps the impressions I received at that former time might be a little modified to-day. Perhaps I should find in Lawrence an exaggeration of methods and effects too closely reminiscent of the school of Reynolds; but his amazing delicacy of drawing, and the air of life he gives to his women, who seem almost to be talking with one, give him, considered as a portrait-painter, a certain superiority over Van Dyck, whose admirable figures are immobile in their pose. Lustrous eyes and parted lips are admirably rendered by Lawrence. He welcomed me with much kindness; he was a man of most charming manners, except when you criticised his pictures.... Our school has need of a little new blood. Our school is old, and the English school seems young. They seem to seek after nature while we busy ourselves with imitating other pictures. Don't get me stoned by mentioning abroad these opinions, which alas! are mine.

Delacroix.

CCXXVI

There are only two occasions, I conceive, on which a foreign artist could with propriety be invited to execute a great national work in this country, namely, in default of our having any artist at all competent to such an undertaking, or for the purpose of introducing a superior style of art, to correct a vicious taste prevalent in the nation. The consideration of the first parts of this statement I leave to those who have witnessed with what ability Mr. Flaxman, Mr. Westmacott, and the other candidates have designed their models, and with respect to the style and good taste of the English school. I dare, and am proud, to assert its superiority over any that has appeared in Europe since the age of the Caracci.

Hoppner.

CCXXVII

(Watts is) the only man who understands great art.

Alfred Stevens.

CCXXVIII

There is only Puvis de Chavannes who holds his place; as for all the others, one must gild their monuments.

Meissonier.

CCXXIX

PRUDHON

In short, he has his own manner; he is the Boucher, the Watteau of our day. We must let him do as he will; it can do no harm at the present time, and in the state the school is in. He deceives himself, but it is not given to every one to deceive themselves like him; his talent has a sure foundation. What I cannot forgive him is that he always draws the same heads, the same arms, and the same hands. All his faces have the same expression, and this expression is always the same grimace. It is not thus we should envisage nature, we who are disciples and admirers of the ancients.

L. David.

CCXXX

ON DELACROIX

Delacroix (except in two pictures, which show a kind of savage genius) is a perfect beast, though almost worshipped here.

Rossetti (1849).

CCXXXI

Delacroix is one of the mighty ones of the earth, and Ingres misses being so creditably.

Rossetti (1856).

CCXXXII

ON DELACROIX

Must I say that I prefer Delacroix with his exaggerations, his mistakes, his obvious falls, because he belongs to no one but himself, because he represents the spirit, the time, and the idiom of his time? Sickly, too highly strung, perhaps, since his art has the melodies of our generation, since in the strained note of his lamentations as in his resounding triumphs, there is always a gasp of the breath, a cry, a fever that are alike our own and his.

We are no longer in the Olympian Age, like Raphael, Veronese, and Rubens; and Delacroix's art is powerful, as a voice from Dante's Inferno.

Rousseau.

CCXXXIII

A DELACROIX EXHIBITION

Feminine painting is invading us; and if our time, of which Delacroix is the true representative, has not dared enough, what will the enervated art of the future be like?

Only paintings are exhibited just now. Two rooms scarcely hold his riches;

and when one thinks that there are here but the elements of Delacroix's production, one is bewildered. What strikes one above all in his sketches is the note of nervous, contained intensity, which during all his full career he never lost; neither fashion nor the influence of others affected it; never was there a more sincere note. Plenty of incorrectness, I grant you, but with a great feeling for drawing. Whatever one may say, if drawing is an instrument of expression, Delacroix was a draughtsman. A great style, a marvellous invention, passion expressed in form as well as in colour, Delacroix is typically the artist, and not a professor of drawing who fills out weakness and mediocrity by rhetoric.

Paul Huet.

CCXXXIV

COROT'S METHOD OF WORK

Corot is a true artist. One must see a painter in his home to have an idea of his merit. I saw again there, and with a quite new appreciation of them, pictures which I had seen at the museum and only cared for moderately. His great "Baptism of Christ" is full of naive beauties; his trees are superb. I asked him about the tree I have to do in the "Orpheus." He told me to walk straight ahead, giving myself up to whatever might come in my way; usually this is what he does. He does not admit that taking infinite pains is lost labour. Titian, Raphael, Rubens, &c., worked easily. They only attempted what they knew; only their range was wider than that of the man who, for instance, only paints landscapes or flowers. Notwithstanding this facility, labour too is indispensable. Corot broods much over things. Ideas come to him, and he adds as he works. It is the right way.

Delacroix.

CCXXXV

From the age of six, I had the passion for drawing the forms of things. By the age of fifty, I had published an infinity of designs; but all that I produced before the age of seventy is of no account. Only when I was seventy-three had I got some sort of insight into the real structure of nature--animals, plants, trees, birds, fish, and insects. Consequently, at the age of eighty I shall have advanced still further; at ninety, I shall grasp the mystery of things; at a hundred, I shall be a marvel, and at a hundred and ten every blot, every line from my brush shall be alive!

Hokusai.

CCXXXVI

It takes an artist fifty years to learn to do anything, and fifty years to learn what not to do--and fifty years to sift and find what he simply desires to do--and 300 years to do it, and when it is done neither heaven nor earth much needs it nor heeds it. Well, I'll peg away; I can do nothing else, and wouldn't if I could.

Burne-Jones.

CCXXXVII

If the Lord lets me live two years longer, I think that I can paint something beautiful.

Corot at 77.

ARS LONGA

CCXXXVIII

If Heaven would give me ten years more ... if Heaven would give me only five years more ... I might become a really great painter.

Hokusai.

CCXXXIX

I will have my Bed to be a Bed of Honour, and cannot die in a better Posture than with my Pencil in my Hand.

Lucas of Leyden.

CCXL

Adieu! I go above to see if friend Corot has found me new landscapes to paint.

Daubigny (on his death-bed).

CCXLI

Leaving my brush in the city of the East, I go to gaze on the divine landscapes of the Paradise of the West.

Hiroshige (on his death-bed).

CCXLII

Much will hereafter be written about subjects and refinements of painting. Sure am I that many notable men will arise, all of whom will write both well and better about this art and will teach it better than I. For I myself hold my art at a very mean value, for I know what my faults are. Let every man therefore strive to better these my errors according to his powers. Would to God it were possible for me to see the work and art of the mighty masters to come, who are yet unborn, for I know that I might be improved. Ah! how often in my sleep do I behold great works of art and beautiful things, the like whereof never appear to me awake, but so soon as I awake even the remembrance of them leaveth me. Let none be ashamed to learn, for a good work requireth good counsel. Nevertheless, whosoever taketh counsel in the arts let him take it from one thoroughly versed in those matters, who can prove what he saith with his hand. Howbeit any one may give thee counsel; and when thou hast done a work pleasing to thyself, it is good for thee to show it to dull men of little judgment that they may give their opinion of it. As a rule, they pick out the most faulty points, whilst they entirely pass over the good. If thou findest something they say true, thou mayest thus better thy work.

Duerer.

CCXLIII

I should be sorry if I had any earthly fame, for whatever natural glory a man has is so much detracted from his spiritual glory. I wish to do nothing for profit; I want nothing; I am quite happy.

Blake.

www.ingramcontent.com/pod-product-compliance
Lightning Source LLC
Chambersburg PA
CBHW050110230526
45470CB00004B/1766